Wrinklies' Wit
and Wisdom

Wrinklies' Wit and Wisdom

Rosemarie Jarski

PRION

First published in 2005 by
Prion
an imprint of the
Carlton Publishing Group
20 Mortimer Street
London W1T 3JW

9 10 8

A catalogue record for this book is available from the British Library

ISBN-10: 1-85375-570-2
ISBN-13: 978-1-85375-570-5

Typeset by e-type, Liverpool
Printed in Great Britain by Mackays

To Mum,

younger than springtime are you

Contents

Introduction 10

Age is Just a Number 15

The Seven Ages of Man 24

Happy Birthday to You? 27

Growing Old 29

When the Pope Starts Looking Young
Signs You're Getting Old 35

Old Age 43

Appearance 48

Dress 58

Hair Today, Gone Tomorrow 61

Eat, Drink and Be Merry ... 64

Exercise 67

Showbiz and Hollywood 70

Music 72

Holding Back the Years 75

The Fountain of Youth 78

Maturity 83

Act Your Age 84

I'm Not Menthyl *Malapropisms* 86

Money 88

Pleasures and Perks of Growing Older 89

Pick More Daisies *Regrets*   105

Mustn't Grumble?   110

Menopause   113

At Least I Have My Health   116

No Medical, and No Salesman Will Call *Insurance*   129

Going Gaga   131

On the Road *Driving*   138

Grandparents and Grandchildren   140

Grandparents Observed   146

Everyone's Favourite Grandmother
Queen Elizabeth, The Queen Mother 1900–2002   150

Parents and Children   155

Twilight Homes for the Bewildered   160

My First 100 Years   161

Secrets of Long Life   163

The Oldest Swinger in Town *Love and Courtship*   169

Marriage   174

Sex   178

Work   186

The Gold Watch *Retirement*   188

Time Flies   192

Carpe Diem   194

Gotta Lotta Livin' To Do   197

A Quiet Life   206

Mind-Lift   209

Silver Surfers *Technology*   210

Age and Youth   212

Mind the Gap *The Generation Gap*   215

The Good Old Days? 217

Life 222

Experience 226

Good and Bad 227

Thank You for Being a Friend *Friendship* 229

Going, Going, Gone! *Death* 231

Excuse My Dust *Epitaph* 245

Afterlife and Immortality 245

Wisdom and Advice 248

Mottoes to Live By 254

With mirth and laughter let old wrinkles come.

William Shakespeare

Introduction

Last year a company which looks into social trends carried out a survey called 'Understanding Fiftysomethings'. Seventeen hundred people, ranging in age from 45 to 89, were questioned about all aspects of their lives. Part of the research invited participants to send in a photograph, 'a snapshot of your life'. On the cover of the final report was a picture of a wheelchair and a Zimmer frame with these words: 'Among 600 snaps taken by older Britons, we found just one like this. So why is it one of the first images to spring to mind when someone mentions old age?' Pictures submitted included a pair of cowboy boots, a computer, a brochure for hip hotels, a pair of Gina high heels, a bottle of wine, and several packets of Rowntree's jelly.

What this reveals – beyond the pleasing fact that a love of jelly lingers on into one's dotage – is the sheer diversity of older people today. Traditional stereotypes of knitting grannies and doddering grandpas just aren't true anymore (if, indeed, they ever were). Older people dress up, drink wine, travel, surf the net, send texts, have sex. The baby-boomer generation has redefined the meaning of 'old'. Grey is the new black! Saga-louts are the new lager-louts! Old is the new young!

Or is it?

Introduction

Old myths die hard. Senior citizens may have changed but the rest of society has yet to notice. The clichéd image of old age is still common currency in our culture. Media and advertising (run by tots barely free of nappy-rash) still lump all older people into one homogenous group. This group is then routinely mocked, trivialized, patronized, or ignored altogether. The over-60s represent over 20 per cent of the population but they feature in only 9 per cent of advertisements and television coverage. The charity Age Concern ran a billboard poster showing the head of a grey-haired man with the caption: 'Ignore this poster. It's got grey hair'. Newspapers and magazines are littered with insidious remarks that undermine or belittle older people. Casual comments like, 'she's on the wrong side of 50', 'he may be in his 60s but …', 'he's still going strong, despite his being 56' may seem innocuous, but multiply them by hundreds of similar comments day after day and they add up to one thing: ageism.

Ageism is entrenched in our society. In the National Health Service, younger patients are up to twice as likely as older ones to receive the best available treatment. Older patients are also more likely to get a DNR – 'Do Not Resuscitate'. The charity Age Concern highlighted the case of an elderly lady who died in hospital and was found to have NFR ('Not For Resuscitation') written across her toes. If this was racism or sexism there would be riots on the streets and questions in Parliament, but because it's 'only old folk' such scandalous treatment elicits barely more than a raised eyebrow.

The test of a civilized society is how it treats its older

citizens. 'It is easy to love children,' writes Abraham Heschel, 'even tyrants and dictators make a point of being fond of children. But the affection and care for the old, the incurable, the helpless are the true gold mines of a culture.' In the United Kingdom, twice as many people give to charities that help animals as those who give to charities supporting older people.

To find respect and deference towards age you have to look beyond Western culture to Asian and African nations. Margaret Simey, a suffragette in the 1920s and local councillor for more than 20 years, was shocked and dismayed to discover that after her retirement she was slung out onto the scrap heap by society and became a non-person. Then she paid a visit to her son in the Southern African kingdom of Lesotho: 'I found myself greeted with enthusiasm by the villagers. Pleased but baffled by my reception, I was told on inquiry that what moved them was their pleasure that my son should enjoy the exceptional good fortune of having such an old mother. To them, my experience and wisdom were worth more than money in the bank.' The Third World has much to teach us about the Third Age.

Similarly, in Japan, reverence for old age is ingrained in their culture and their psyche. As Barbara Bloom observes: 'When the Japanese mend broken objects they aggrandize the damage by filling the cracks with gold, because they believe that when something's suffered damage and has a history it becomes more beautiful.'

Any society that doesn't value its older citizens is off its rocker. We're all getting older so ageism is like turkeys voting for Christmas. Ignorance and fear are at the root of it. Dread of our own deterioration and mortality leads to fear and revulsion of old people who are reminders of that inevitability.

Making role models of celebrities doesn't help. None fear the ageing process more than they. Celebrities may pay collagen-enhanced-lip-service to growing old gracefully, but then they sneak off to the plastic surgeon's to be nipped, tucked and liposuctioned to within an inch of their livers. They line up to go on *Oprah* to share their drink, drug and sex addictions but how many will 'fess up to a facelift? There's a saying in Hollywood: 'The second worst sin is to be old; the worst is to look old.' The mother of Zsa Zsa Gabor was still having cosmetic surgery in her 90s. Before going under the knife she instructed her surgeon to complete the procedure even if she died on the operating table.

Let's face it, when it comes to ageing, our society needs to fundamentally rethink its attitudes – and fast. Advances in preventative medicine and improved nutrition mean we're staying healthy and living longer. By 2030, one third of the entire population of the UK will be over 60. Centenarians are the world's fastest-growing age group, and scientists predict that millennium babies can expect to live to be 130.

Great news. But what's the point of these extra years if all we can look forward to are discrimination, derision and yet more adverts for life insurance ('no medical, and no salesman will call')? Life is not just about staying alive but *living*. What we need are better role models, less hypocrisy, more honesty, an end to the obsession with youth, an education programme to teach the younger generation to value experience and wisdom, and a more accurate reflection of what life is like after the free bus pass.

A collection of wrinklies' wit and wisdom can't change the world; the best it can do is to fly the flag for wrinklies everywhere. Gilded youth is swept aside as golden oldies take centre-stage. But that's not to say that the young can't also find enjoyment – and enlightenment – here. This is a book for anyone who's getting older. John Mortimer, The Golden Girls, Barry Cryer, Bill Crosby and Elaine Stritch are inspirational role models for any age. They never pass their amuse-by dates; their wisdom is timeless. Most of the contributors can ride the buses for free so they speak with the voice of experience. They shoot from the hip – real or titanium – sharing the pleasures as well as what Byron called 'the woes that wait on age'. Wrapping those woes in wit doesn't make them go away but it does make them a bit more bearable. If laughter is the best medicine, consider this the perfect prescription for ageing well and living a full and happy life. Pop a few pearls of wit and wisdom every day and that telegram from Her Majesty is practically in the bag. You see, he who laughs, lasts.

Age is Just a Number

I'm very pleased to be here. Let's face it, at my age I'm pleased to be anywhere.

George Burns

He was either a man of about 150 who was rather young for his years, or a man of about 110 who had been aged by trouble.

P.G. Wodehouse

I'm as old as my tongue and a little bit older than my teeth.

Kris Kringle, Miracle on 34th Street

Age is a question of mind over matter. If you don't mind, age don't matter.

Satchel Paige

We're obsessed with age. Numbers are always and pointlessly attached to every name that's published in a newspaper: 'Joe Creamer, 43, and his daughter, Tiffany-Ann, 9, were merrily chasing a bunny, 2, when Tiffany-Ann tripped on the root of a tree, 106.'

Joan Rivers

Wrinklies' Wit and Wisdom

People who define themselves by their age are about as appealing to be with as feminists who drone on about women's rights, homosexuals who are obsessed with being gay, or environmentalists who mention recycling every time they drop by for green tea.

Marcelle D'Argy-Smith

Exactly how old is Joan Collins? We need an expert. Someone who counts the rings on trees.

Ruby Wax

Let's just say I reached the age of consent 75,000 consents ago.

Shelley Winters

My sister, Jackie, is younger than me. We don't know quite by how much.

Joan Collins

I don't know how old I am because the goat ate the Bible that had my birth certificate in it. The goat lived to be 27.

Satchel Paige

Age is something that doesn't matter, unless you are a cheese.

Billie Burke

Age is Just a Number

Age only matters when one is ageing. Now that I have arrived at a great age, I might just as well be 20.

Pablo Picasso

I'm 80, but in my own mind, my age veers. When I'm performing on stage, I'm 40; when I'm shopping in Waitrose, I'm 120.

Humphrey Lyttelton

I'm 42 around the chest, 52 around the waist, 92 around the golf course and a nuisance around the house.

Groucho Marx

When I turned 2 I was really anxious, because I'd doubled my age in a year. I thought, if this keeps up, by the time I'm 6 I'll be 90.

Steven Wright

How old would you be if you didn't know how old you were?

Satchel Paige

I have no romantic feelings about age. Either you are interesting at any age or you are not. There is nothing particularly interesting about being old – or being young, for that matter.

Katharine Hepburn

Wrinklies' Wit and Wisdom

'When I was your age …' No one is ever anyone else's age, except physically.

Faith Baldwin

It is a sobering thought that when Mozart was my age he had been dead for two years.

Tom Lehrer

I am just turning 40 and taking my time about it.

Harold Lloyd, 77

I can't believe I'm 30. Do you know how much that is in gay years?

Jack McFarland, Will and Grace

I am past 30, and three parts iced over.

Matthew Arnold

If you want to know how old a woman is, ask her sister-in-law.

Ed Howe

I refuse to admit that I'm more than 52, even if that does make my sons illegitimate.

Nancy Astor

The years that a woman subtracts from her age are not lost. They are added to the ages of other women.

Diane de Poitiers

I can lie convincingly about my age because at my age I can't always remember what it is.

Violet Conti

When I hit 55 I decided to start telling people I was older so they would compliment me on how young I looked for my age. But I was hoist by my own petard when the first person I told I was 60 laid a sympathetic hand on my shoulder and said, 'Not to worry, we old timers must stick together!'

Lydia Martinez

Thirty is a nice age for a woman. Especially if she happens to be 40.

Phyllis Diller

A woman telling her true age is like a buyer confiding his final price to an Armenian rug dealer.

Mignon McLaughlin

I have always felt that a woman has the right to treat the subject of her age with ambiguity until, perhaps, she passes into the realm beyond 90. Then it is better that she be candid with herself and with the world.

Helena Rubinstein

Wrinklies' Wit and Wisdom

Never trust a woman who tells one her real age. A woman who would tell one that, would tell anything.

Oscar Wilde

A woman is as old as she looks before breakfast.

Ed Howe

She may very well pass for 43 in the dusk with the light behind her!

W.S. Gilbert

If the Nobel Prize were awarded by a woman, it would go to the inventor of the dimmer switch.

Kathy Lette

– Age is nothing but a state of mind.
– Tell that to my thighs.

Dorothy Zbornak and Blanche Devereaux, The Golden Girls

A woman is as young as her knees.

Mary Quant

People who say you're just as old as you feel are all wrong, fortunately.

Russell Baker

The best thing to do is to behave in a manner befitting one's age. If you are 16 or under, try not to go bald.

Woody Allen

The worst thing anyone has ever said about me is that I'm 50. Which I am. Oh that bitch. I was so hurt.

Joan Rivers

The real sadness of being 50 is not that you change so much but that you change so little.

Max Lerner

Whenever the talk turns to age, I say I am 49 plus VAT.

Lionel Blair

The years between 50 and 70 are the hardest. You are always being asked to do things, and you are not yet decrepit enough to turn them down.

T.S. Eliot

I'm 52 years of age now but I prefer to think of myself as 11 centigrade.

Tom Lehrer

The war years count double. Things and people not actively in use age twice as fast.

Arnold Bennett

Wrinklies' Wit and Wisdom

I recently turned 60. Practically a third of my life is over.

Woody Allen

I have been a success: for 60 years I have eaten, and have avoided being eaten.

Logan Pearsall Smith

Here I sit, alone and 60, bald and fat and full of sin; cold the seat and loud the cistern, as I read the Harpic tin.

Alan Bennett

At the end of this year, I shall be 63 – if alive – and about the same if dead.

Mark Twain

Will you still need me, will you still feed me, when I'm 64?

Paul McCartney & John Lennon

I'm 65, but if there were 15 months in every year I'd only be 48.

James Thurber

I'll never make the mistake of turning 70 again.

Casey Stengel

Age is Just a Number

It is better to be 70 years young than 40 years old.

Oliver Wendell Holmes

If it's true that 50 is the new 30, then it follows that 70 is the new 50.

Joan Collins

You don't realize what fine fighting material there is in age. You show me anyone who's lived to over 70 and you show me a fighter – someone who's got the will to live.

Agatha Christie

I'm 78. The late Ronnie Scott used to ask people their age and would respond, in his hard-edged way: 'Really! You don't look a day over (in my case) 79!' A good corrective, which I resort to when I feel sorry for myself.

George Melly

Eighty's a landmark and people treat you differently than they do when you're 79. At 79, if you drop something it just lies there. At 80, people pick it up for you.

Helen Van Slyke

In a dream you are never 80.

Anne Sexton

There must be a day or two in a man's life when he is the precise age for something important.

Franklin Pierce Adams

The life expectancy now is 72 for men, and 75 or 76 or something for women. It's amazing to think that just a couple thousand years ago, life expectancy was 30, which in our terms would be that you get your driver's licence around 5, get married at 9, divorced at 15, in your late teens you move down to Florida.

Jerry Seinfeld

If a Renaissance or Georgian man could return he would be as much astonished by the sight of two or three thousand septuagenarians and octogenarians lining a south-coast resort on a summer's day, as he would by a television set. His was a world where it was the exception to be grey.

Ronald Blythe

The Seven Ages of Man

The seven ages of man have become preschooler, Pepsi generation, baby boomer, mid-lifer, empty-nester, senior citizen, and organ donor.

Bill Cosby

The three ages of man: youth, middle age, and 'You're looking wonderful!'

Dore Schary

There are three stages of man: he believes in Santa Claus; he does not believe in Santa Claus; he is Santa Claus.

Bob Phillips

There are only three ages for women in Hollywood: Babe, District Attorney, and Driving Miss Daisy.

Goldie Hawn

Your 40s, you grow a little potbelly, you grow another chin. The music starts to get too loud and one of your old girlfriends from high school becomes a grandmother. Your 50s you have a minor surgery. You'll call it a procedure, but it's a surgery. Your 60s you have a major surgery, the music is still loud but it doesn't matter because you can't hear it anyway. 70s, you and the wife retire to Fort Lauderdale, you start eating dinner at 2, lunch around 10, breakfast the night before. And you spend most of your time wandering around malls looking for the ultimate in soft yoghurt and muttering 'How come the kids don't call?' By your 80s, you've had a major

stroke, and you end up babbling to some
Jamaican nurse who your wife can't stand but
who you call mama. Any questions?

Mitch Robbins, City Slickers

My mother used to say the seven ages were:
childhood, adolescence, adulthood, middle age,
elderly, old, and wonderful.

Mary Wilson

I think the life cycle is all backwards. You should
die first, get it out of the way. Then you live in
an old age home. You get kicked out when
you're too young, you get a gold watch, you go
to work. You work 40 years until you're young
enough to enjoy your retirement. You do drugs,
alcohol, you party, you get ready for high
school. You go to grade school, you become a
kid, you play, you have no responsibilities, you
become a little baby, you go back into the
womb, you spend your last 9 months floating …
and you finish off as an orgasm.

George Carlin

Be on the alert to recognize your prime at
whatever time of your life it may occur.

Miss Jean Brodie, The Prime of Miss Jean Brodie,
Muriel Spark

It has begun to occur to me that life is a stage I'm going through.

Ellen Goodman

Happy Birthday to You?

Two weeks ago we celebrated my uncle's 103rd birthday. 103 – isn't that something? Unfortunately he wasn't present. How could he be? He died when he was 29.

Victor Borge

Like a hole in the head I need another birthday.

Dorothy Parker

For all the advances in medicine, there is still no cure for the common birthday.

John Glenn

A diplomat is a man who always remembers a woman's birthday but never remembers her age.

Robert Frost

Birthdays are nature's way of telling us to eat more cake.

Jo Brand

Wrinklies' Wit and Wisdom

Birthdays are good for you. Statistics show that the people who have the most live the longest.

Larry Lorenzoni

I had a huge party for my 70th birthday with 800 guests. With so many familiar faces there, it was like driving through the rear-view mirror.

Peter Ustinov

Buying presents for old people is a problem. I would rather like it if people came to my house and took things away.

Clement Freud

I was invited to Hugh Hefner's 75th birthday party but I couldn't figure out what gift to buy him. What do you give the man who's had everyone? Then I thought of it: monogrammed Viagra!

David Letterman

What would I like for my 87th birthday? A paternity suit.

George Burns

– Be honest, Victor, I bet this was the last birthday present you were expecting?
– Yes, it was. It's ermmm…a gravestone.

– Yes. You haven't already got one? Obviously
I haven't filled in the date of death yet, but if
and when – Margaret can just give me a
shout.

George and Victor Meldrew, One Foot in the Grave

Last week the candle factory burned down.
Everyone just stood around and sang Happy
Birthday.

Steven Wright

Growing Old

– You know what the worst part about getting
old is?
– Your face?

Blanche Devereaux and Dorothy Zbornak,
The Golden Girls

Growing old is like being increasingly penalized
for a crime you haven't committed.

Anthony Powell

Age to women is like Kryptonite to Superman.

Kathy Lette

Wrinklies' Wit and Wisdom

There is absolutely nothing to be said in favour of growing old. There ought to be legislation against it.

Patrick Moore

In the middle of the 19th century, an Englishman named Robert Browning wrote: 'Grow old along with me, the best is yet to be.' Clearly this man was a minor poet. Or else he wrote those lines when he was 12.

Joan Rivers

I am not 'of a certain age', Niles. I am smack dab in the middle of 'not a kid anymore'. I won't be 'of a certain age' for another 10 years.

Frasier Crane, Frasier

Frasier, you may think it's tough being middle aged but think about me – I've got a son who's middle aged.

Martin Crane, Frasier

Middle age is when you're sitting at home on Saturday night and the telephone rings and you hope it isn't for you.

Ogden Nash

I am at that age. Too young for the bowling green, too old for Ecstasy.

Rab C. Nesbitt

One problem with growing older is that it gets increasingly tougher to find a famous historical figure who didn't amount to much when he was your age.

Bill Vaughan

There are days of oldness, and then one gets young again. It goes backward and forward, not in one direction.

Katharine Hathaway

People want you to be like you were in 1969. They want you to be, because otherwise their youth goes with you.

Mick Jagger

Only two things improve with age: wine and Susan Sarandon.

Boyd Farrow

Jameson's Irish Whiskey really does improve with age: the older I get the more I like it.

Bob Monkhouse

When I was elected to the European Parliament, I was invited to join its Committee on Ageing. The very words put years on me and I refused, saying that the only committee in which I might be interested would be a committee on keeping young.

Barbara Castle

I don't believe that one grows older. I think that what happens early on in life is that at a certain age one stands still and stagnates.

T.S. Eliot

There are people whose watch stops at a certain hour and who remain permanently at that age.

Charles Augustin Sainte-Beuve

Many people die at 25 and aren't buried until they are 75.

Max Frisch

Colleagues of Margaret Thatcher have rejected criticism that she is now a pale reflection of her former self because, as they recall it, she never had a reflection.

Dead Ringers

Growing Old

Growing old is no more than a bad habit which a busy man has not time to form.

André Maurois

When friends pressed her to carry a walking stick, Princess Alice reluctantly agreed, but she had it disguised as an umbrella.

R. W. Apple

She had finally reached the age where she was more afraid of getting old than dying.

Julia Phillips

Why do we get older? Why do our bodies wear out? Why can't we just go on and on, accumulating a potentially infinite number of Frequent Flier mileage points?

Dave Barry

I'm 43, and for the first time this year I have felt older. I'm slowly becoming more decrepit. I think you just move to the country and wear an old fleece.

Jennifer Saunders

Old age and sickness bring out the essential characteristics of a man.

Felix Frankfurter

It's sad to grow old, but nice to ripen.

Brigitte Bardot

The best way to adjust – no, ignore – most of the negative thoughts about ageing is to say to yourself, with conviction, 'I am still the *very same* person I have been all of my adult life.' You *are*, you know.

Helen Hayes

A good old age can be the crown of our life's experience, the masterwork of a lifetime.

Helen Nearing

Oh, I was so much older then; I'm younger than that now.

Bob Dylan

Growing old is something you do if you're lucky.

Groucho Marx

When the Pope Starts Looking Young

SIGNS YOU'RE GETTING OLD

There are three signs of old age: loss of memory … I forget the other two.

Red Skelton

You will recognize, my boy, the first sign of old age: it is when you go out into the streets of London and realize for the first time how young the policemen look.

Seymour Hicks

Do you think policemen walk up and down the street thinking how old the public are getting these days?

D. Tucker

You know you're getting old when high court judges start looking young to you.

Ronnie Golden

I knew I was getting old when the Pope started looking young.

Billy Wilder

Wrinklies' Wit and Wisdom

An uncle of mine, a retired headmaster, said that the first time he felt old was when he was in a queue at his local post office to collect his old age pension and found himself behind a former pupil who was there for the same purpose.

Paul Kelvin-Smith

True terror is to wake up one morning and discover that your high school class is running the country.

Kurt Vonnegut

Whenever a man's friends begin to compliment him about looking young, he may be sure that they think he is growing old.

Washington Irving

I was in a coffee shop doing a survey for free drinks. The age bracket tick boxes were: 16–21; 21–27; 27–35; 35–50. I am over 50 and I realized I am one tick box away from death.

Anon

A British Gas salesman, replacing a defective boiler, told me: 'The makers will tell you this boiler will give 25 years' service.' He looked up at me, hesitated, and continued, 'But of course to you that would not be a selling point.'

Kenneth Bruce, 78

When the Pope Starts Looking Young

I've started wearing cardigans and saying things like 'Whoopsadaisy', and when I take a first sip of tea, 'Ooh, that hits the spot!'

Gary, Men Behaving Badly

If, at the age of 30, you are stiff and out of shape, then you are old. If, at 60, you are supple and strong, then you are young.

Joseph Pilates

Signs you're getting on a bit: your back hurts; you eat food past its sell-by date; your carpet is patterned; you go supermarket shopping in the evening to pick up marked-down bargains; you can spell; you hang your clothes on padded coat hangers; you save the hearing aid flyer that falls out of the colour supplement; you try to get electrical gadgets repaired when they go wrong; you save the free little packets of sugar from cafés; you have worn a knitted swimsuit; when you watch black and white films you spend the whole time pointing at the screen going, 'He's dead … She's dead …'; your car stereo is tuned to Radio 2.

Colin Slater

You know you're getting older if you have more fingers than real teeth.

Rodney Dangerfield

Wrinklies' Wit and Wisdom

One of the signs of old age is that you have to carry your senses around in your handbag – glasses, hearing aid, dentures, etc.

Kurt Strauss

I contemplated buying a new cream that claimed to stop the 7 signs of ageing and wondered what they might be. Incontinence? Talking about the weather? Wearing slippers? Memory loss? Compulsive need to queue up at the post office? Memory loss? Inability to comprehend the lyrics of pop songs?

Maria McErlane

I first felt old walking in Spain with my 13-year-old daughter when I belatedly realized the wolf-whistle was not for me.

Adele Thorpe

I know I must be getting old because I saw a young lady with her midriff showing and thought, 'Ooh, you must be cold.'

John Marsh

You know you're getting old when you feel like the day after the night before and you haven't even been anywhere.

Milton Berle

When the Pope Starts Looking Young

You know you're knocking on when you get to the top of the stairs and can't remember what you went up for. So you go back downstairs to help you remember what you went upstairs for. You finally remember what you went upstairs for so up you go again but when you find it you have forgotten why you wanted it.

Millicent Kemp

You know you're getting older when the first thing you do after you're done eating is look for a place to lie down.

Louie Anderson

A young boy down the road tried to help me across the road this afternoon. I gave him a swift cuff round the ear. Only be a matter of time before they're forcing me on a day trip to Eastbourne.

Victor Meldrew, One Foot in the Grave

You know you're getting old when you go on holiday and always pack a sweater.

Denis Norden

You're getting old when you stop loving snow and sweetcorn.

Susan H. Llewellyn

Wrinklies' Wit and Wisdom

You know you're getting old when you and your partner wear matching sweaters.

Mark Schofield

I know I'm getting older because these days, before I leave in the morning, I have to ask myself, 'Did I remember to pluck my ears?'

Christopher Moore

You know you're getting old when you open the fridge door and can't remember if you're putting something in or taking something out.

Lottie Robson

You know you're getting old when your grown children get you as a present one of those stupid books about 'the joys of ageing'.

Garrison Keillor

You know you're getting old when you turn out the light for economic reasons instead of romantic ones.

Herbert J. Kavet

You know you're getting on when you start getting symptoms in the places you used to get urges.

Denis Norden

When the Pope Starts Looking Young

You know you're getting old when you don't notice the smell any more when the toast burns.

Ron Jowker

You know you're getting old when you're dashing through Marks and Spencer's, spot a pair of Dr Scholl's sandals, stop, and think, hmm, they look comfy.

Victoria Wood

You know you're getting old when you're no longer offered a puff of the latest perfume at the department store.

Rowena Kemp

You know you're getting old when your wife believes your excuses for getting home late.

Basil Ransome-Davies

You know you're old when your family talk about you in front of you. What are we going to do with Pop? We have company tonight.

Rodney Dangerfield

Being old is getting up in the middle of the night as often as George Clooney, but not for the same reason.

Mel Brooks

Twice Nightly Whiteley? Sometimes it's *Thrice* Nightly Whiteley. That man is a martyr to his bladder.

Kathyrn Apanowicz, partner of Richard Whiteley

You know you're getting old when you're interested in going home before you get where you're going.

Alan Mainwaring

A man knows he is growing old because he begins to look like his father.

Gabriel García Márquez

You know you're getting old when you start to like your mum and dad again. 'Yes, mum, I'd love to come caravanning to Tenby with you. No, I'll bring a packed lunch. I'm not paying café prices.'

Jeff Green

You know you're getting old when a 4-letter word for something pleasurable two people can do in bed is R-E-A-D.

Denis Norden

You know you're getting old when you stoop to tie your shoelaces and wonder what else you can do while you're down there.

George Burns

Old Age

At a church social, a little boy came up and asked me how old I was. I said, 'I'm 76.' 'And you're still alive?' he said.

Jack Wilson

Alive in the sense that he can't legally be buried.

Geoffrey Madan

– Smithers, what's my password?
– It's your age, sir.
– Excellent! [*4 beeps are heard*]

Mr Burns and Smithers, The Simpsons

– I'm a college professor. What did you think when I said I taught Hemingway?
– I thought you were old.

Miles Webber and Rose Martin, The Golden Girls

I'm so old that when I order a 3-minute egg, they ask for the money up front.

Milton Berle

I'm so old I daren't even buy green bananas.

Bruce Forsyth

Wrinklies' Wit and Wisdom

I'm at an age when if I drop a fiver in the collection plate, it's not a donation, it's an investment.

Ralph Layton

Anyone can get old. All you have to do is to live long enough.

Groucho Marx

How do you know when you're old? When you double your current age and realize you're not going to live that long.

Michael Leyden

I'm 59 and people call me middle aged. How many 118-year-old men do you know?

Barry Cryer

Old age is like waiting in the departure lounge of life. Fortunately, we are in England and the train is bound to be late.

Milton Shulman

You are as young as your faith, as old as your doubt; as young as your self-confidence, as old as your fear; as young as your hope, as old as your despair.

Douglas MacArthur

I hope I never get so old I get religious.

Ingmar Bergman

Old age is not for sissies.

Bette Davis

I don't know how you feel about old age, but in my case I didn't even see it coming. It hit me from the rear.

Phyllis Diller

The ageing process is not gradual or gentle. It rushes up, pushes you over and runs off laughing. Dying is a matter of slapstick and prat falls.

John Mortimer

Old age is like underwear. It creeps up on you.

Lois L. Kaufman

Old age is the most unexpected of all things that happen to a man.

Leon Trotsky

A person is always startled when he hears himself called an old man for the first time.

Oliver Wendell Holmes

I do what I can to help the elderly; after all, I'm going to be old myself some day.

Lillian Carter, 76

Wrinklies' Wit and Wisdom

The older I get, the older old is.

Tom Baker

To me, old age is always 15 years older than I am.

Bernard Baruch

I'm Too Young to be This Old

Slogan on a senior citizen's T-shirt

Inside yourself, you're still the same age as you were when you were 11. It's just that various bits keep dropping off.

John Mortimer

I don't feel old. In fact I don't feel anything until noon. Then it's time for my nap.

Bob Hope

Old age is when you know all the answers, but nobody asks you the questions.

Laurence J. Peter

Old age is realizing you will never own all the dogs you wanted to.

Joe Gores

Old age is a time of life when the phone rings less often, but more ominously.

Edmund Volkart

Old is when your wife says, 'Let's go upstairs and make love,' and you answer, 'Honey, I can't do both.'

Red Buttons

Old age is a lot of crossed-off names in your address book.

Ronald Blythe

W.C. Fields has a profound respect for old age. Especially when it's bottled.

Gene Fowler

Every age can be enchanting, provided you live within it.

Brigitte Bardot

Women never have young minds. They are born 3,000 years old.

Shelagh Delaney

There is no old age. There is, as there always was, just you.

Carol Matthau

Old age is like a plane flying through a storm. Once you are aboard there is nothing you can do about it. So one might as well accept it calmly, wisely.

Golda Meir

There's one more terrifying fact about old people: I'm going to be one soon.

P.J. O'Rourke

Old age isn't so bad when you consider the alternative.

Maurice Chevalier

Appearance

– Good afternoon, I'm Dorothy Zbornak.
– Geriatrics is two doors down on the left.

Dorothy Zbornak and Hospital Receptionist, Empty Nest

There is a saying, 'Youth is a gift of nature; Age is a work of art.' If age is a work of art, the artist is one who belongs on the subway and not in the Louvre.

Bill Cosby

As I rose from my bath, I caught sight of myself in the mirror. I suddenly saw a great white sea monster emerging out of the water. This enormous sub-aquatic creature could not possibly be me, could it?

Julian Fellowes

Appearance

I still think of myself as I was 25 years ago. Then I look in the mirror and see an old bastard and I realize it's me.

Dave Allen

Let us be grateful to the mirror for revealing to us our appearance only.

Samuel Butler

It is 11 years since I have seen my figure in a mirror: the last reflection I saw there was so disagreeable I resolved to spare myself such mortification in the future, and shall continue that resolution to my life's end.

Lady Mary Wortley Montagu

Sometimes I catch a glimpse of my outward self reflected in a shop window and see my mother. That old woman can't be me!

Prue Phillipson

A while ago I asked John Clarke to give us a talk here at Knapely Women's Institute. Annie asked me to read it to you here tonight, and this is what he wrote: 'The flowers of Yorkshire are like the women of Yorkshire. Every stage of their growth has its own beauty, but the last phase is always the most glorious. Then very quickly they all go to seed.'

Chris, Calendar Girls

Wrinklies' Wit and Wisdom

If you really want to annoy your glamorous, well-preserved 42-year-old auntie, say, 'I bet you were really pretty when you were young.'

Lily Savage

Twenty-four years ago, Madam, I was incredibly handsome. The remains of it are still visible through the rift of time. I was so handsome that women became spellbound when I came in view. In San Francisco, in rainy seasons, I was frequently mistaken for a cloudless day.

Mark Twain

After a certain number of years, our faces become our biographies.

Cynthia Ozick

Eric Sykes is about to be 79. He has the stretching, slowly inquiring, slightly doomy head of one of those lovely, ancient sea turtles you see on wildlife programmes.

Deborah Ross

An old man looks permanent, as if he had been born an old man.

H.E. Bates

I have reached the age when I look just as good standing on my head as I do right side up.

Frank Sullivan

Appearance

Jesus! Look at my hands. Now really, I am too young for liver spots. Maybe I can merge them into a tan.

Diane, September

I swear I'm ageing about as well as a beach-party movie.

Harvey Fierstein, Torch Song Trilogy

I beg your pardon, I didn't recognize you – I've changed a lot.

Oscar Wilde

Do I look older? Look at my face, sweetie? What do you see? You may lie, darling, I'm just looking for a response.

Edina Monsoon, Absolutely Fabulous

I've got enough crow's feet to start a bird sanctuary.

Kathy Lette

After a certain age, a woman should never leave the house.

Jennifer Jones

I've often thought that the ageing process could be slowed down if it had to work its way through Parliament.

Edwina Currie

Wrinklies' Wit and Wisdom

First I was 'pretty'. Now I'm 'interesting – got character'. Soon I'll be 'handsome' and then, worst of all, I'll be 'remarkable for my age'.

Valerie Harper, Chapter Two

I didn't want to look my age, but I didn't want to act the age I wanted to look either. I also wanted to grow old enough to understand that sentence.

Erma Bombeck

As long as a woman can look 10 years younger than her own daughter, she is perfectly satisfied.

Oscar Wilde

My looks had gone by the age of 7.

Dodie Smith

Walking past a building site on my way to the shops, I was wolf-whistled by a hunky construction worker on some scaffolding. I'm 63. It made my day.

Janet Lynn

You can be glamorous at any age. It is *not* the prerogative of the young. In fact, the self-confidence of experience is an added bonus.

Joan Collins

Sex appeal is 50 per cent what you've got and 50 per cent what people think you've got.

Sophia Loren

Cut off my head and I am 13.

Coco Chanel, 60

Good cheekbones are the brassiere of old age.

Barbara de Portago

So much has been said and sung of beautiful young girls, why doesn't somebody wake up to the beauty of old women?

Harriet Beecher Stowe

No spring, nor summer beauty hath such grace, As I have seen in one autumnal face.

John Donne, 'The Autumnal' Elegy

She had accomplished what according to builders is only possible to wood and stone of the very finest grain; she had *weathered*, as they call it, with beauty.

Ethel Smyth

I won't ever feel old, and I won't ever look old because I'm a cartoon – like Mickey Mouse.

Dolly Parton

Wrinklies' Wit and Wisdom

I'm at that age when everything Mother Nature gave me, Father Time is taking away.

George Burns

When I go upstairs my buttocks applaud me and my knees sound like potato chips.

Joan Rivers

Women are not forgiven for ageing. Robert Redford's 'lines of distinction' are my 'old-age wrinkles'.

Jane Fonda

There are new lines on my face. I look like a brand new, steel-belted radial tyre.

Diana Barrie, California Suite

If God had to give a woman wrinkles He might at least have put them on the soles of her feet.

Ninon de Lenclos

One thing to be said for wrinkles – at least they don't hurt.

Betty Smith

Keep looking at my eyes, dahling. My arse is like an accordion.

Tallulah Bankhead

It's hard to be devil-may-care when there are pleats in your derrière.

Judith Viorst

I said to my husband, my boobs have gone, my stomach's gone, say something nice about my legs. He said, 'Blue goes with everything.'

Joan Rivers

Mick Jagger told me the wrinkles on his face were laughter lines, but nothing is that funny.

George Melly

When I looked at the wrinkled skin on W.H. Auden's face, I kept wondering, what must his balls look like?

David Hockney

I'm not really wrinkled. I just took a nap on a chenille bedspread.

Phyllis Diller

Wrinklies' Wit and Wisdom

— I haven't got bad boobs for a woman of my age.
— Behave, Barbara, they're like bloody spaniels' ears.

Barbara and Jim Royle, The Royle Family

I have everything I had 20 years ago, only now it's 6 inches lower.

Gypsy Rose Lee

Whenever I see some floozy in a boob tube I scream, 'Listen, honey, even the Roman Empire fell, and those things will too.'

Phyllis Diller

Thirty years ago I got a tattoo of the yellow rose of Texas and green leaf, right above my heart. But with age comes sagging, and my yellow rose of Texas is now down to my waist and looks like a picture of Tony Bennett with liver disease and an elf hat.

Sally Jackson

I no longer have upper arms. I have wing span.

Bette Midler

You are rapidly approaching the age when your body, whether it embarrasses you or not, begins to embarrass other people.

Alan Bennett, Getting On

Fat people don't seem to age as much as thin people, not when you get close up and inspect the damage.

Hunter Davies

After 40 a woman has to choose between losing her figure or her face. My advice is to keep your face, and stay sitting down.

Barbara Cartland

Nature gives you the face you have at 20. Life shapes the face you have at 30. But at 50 you get the face you deserve.

Coco Chanel

There are people who are beautiful in dilapidation, like houses that were hideous when new.

Logan Pearsall Smith

Like all ruins, I look best by moonlight. Give me a sprig of ivy and an owl under my arm and Tintern Abbey would not be in it with me.

W.S. Gilbert

The paint and plaster may be peeling and cracking on the outside but that doesn't matter if the rooms inside are warm and cosy.

Anon

Dress

Dorothy, was Sophia naked just now or does her dress really need ironing?

Rose Nylund, The Golden Girls

Men in the uniform of Wall Street retirement: black Chesterfield coat, rimless glasses and *The Times* folded to the obituary page.

Jimmy Breslin

Inspired by the line in Jenny Joseph's poem 'Warning' that vows, 'When I am an old woman, I shall wear purple, with a red hat that doesn't go', I started 'The Red Hat Society'. It's for women who want to grow old playfully.

Sue Ellen Cooper

Never wear grey. Wearing grey makes one feel grey. I was shown round Tutankhamun's tomb in the 1920s. I saw all this wonderful pink on the walls and the artefacts. I was so impressed that I vowed to wear it for the rest of my life.

Barbara Cartland

– Dorothy, do you think I'm dressed okay for the dog races?
– That depends – are you competing?

Blanche Devereaux and Sophia Petrillo, The Golden Girls

My mother buys me those big granny panties, 3 in a pack. You can use them for a car cover.

Monique Marvez

Caesar had his toga, Adam had his leaf, but when I wear a thong it gives my piles such grief.

Sandra Mayhew

My dad's trousers kept creeping up on him. By the time he was 65, he was just a pair of pants and a head.

Jeff Altman

I have never seen an old person in a new bathing suit in my life. I don't know where they get their bathing suits, but my father has bathing suits from other centuries. If I forget mine, he always wants me to wear his.

Jerry Seinfeld

Wrinklies' Wit and Wisdom

I'm a child of the Sixties. I still wear jeans and yes, my bum looks big in them but then my bum looked big in 1965.

Julia Richardson

I can see nothing wrong with 40-, 50-, or 60-year-old men dressing and acting like teenagers. I'm an elderly man of 44 and, after a few miserable years of being sensible, I do it all the time.

Jeremy Clarkson

A sign your best years are behind you is when you slip into your first pair of slippers. They smack of smugness and a grisly domesticity.

Piers Hernu

Roll carpet slippers in breadcrumbs, bake until golden brown, then tell friends you're wearing Findus Crispy Pancakes.

H. Lloyd, Top Tip, Viz

At 50, confine your piercings to sardine cans.

Joan Rivers

– Now, if you'll excuse me, I'm going to slip into something that will make me look my best.
– May I suggest a time-machine?

Blanche Devereaux and Sophia Petrillo, The Golden Girls

Hair Today, Gone Tomorrow

I found my first grey hair today. On my chest.
Wendy Liebman

A wonderful woman my grandmother – 86 years old and not a single grey hair on her head. She's completely bald.
Les Dawson

When men get grey hair, they look distinguished. When women get grey hair, they look old. When women get breasts, they look sexy. When men get breasts, they look old.
Dick Solomon

Grey-haired men look 'distinguished'? Surely the word is 'extinguished'.
Julie Burchill

I'm so grey, I look like I'm gonna rain sometimes. And my pubic hair is going grey. In a certain light you'd swear it was Stewart Granger down there.
Billy Connolly

I used to think I'd like less grey hair. Now I'd like more of it.
Richie Benaud

I knew I was going bald when it was taking longer and longer to wash my face.

Harry Hill

The method preferred by most balding men for making themselves look silly is called the 'comb-over', which is when the man grows the hair on one side of his head very long and combs it across the bald area, creating an effect that looks from the top like an egg in the grasp of a large tropical spider.

Dave Barry

Men going bald is Nature's way of stopping them having any more crap hairstyles.

Tony, Men Behaving Badly

Peter Stringfellow's hairstyle is older than some of his girlfriends.

Paul Merton

There's one good thing about being bald: it's neat.

Milton Berle

The most delightful advantage of being bald – one can *hear* snowflakes.

R. G. Daniels

Hair Today, Gone Tomorrow

I love bald men. Just because you've lost your fuzz doesn't mean you ain't a peach.

Dolly Parton

Over the years, I've tried a variety of ways to regain my hair. I had shots of oestrogen in my scalp. I didn't grow any hair – but I went up a cup size.

Tony Kornheiser

– Do you think she's wearing a wig?
– Yes, definitely, but it's a very good one. You'd never guess.

Two old ladies overheard on a bus

People ask me how long it takes to do my hair. I don't know, I'm never there.

Dolly Parton

The hair is real. It's the head that's fake.

Steve Allen

His toupee makes him look 20 years sillier.

Bill Dana

If that thing had legs it'd be a rat.

Martin Kemp

Things For Guys to Consider Before Buying a Hairpiece: Will it appreciate in value? Is it possible a hairpiece will make me look too good? Will I be able to handle all the women? Have I explored *all* my comb-over options?

David Letterman

– Hi, Stan. Where's your hair?
– Oh damn, I should have never let the sun roof down.

Rose Nylund and Stan Zbornak, The Golden Girls

Wig wearers! Secure your toupee in high winds by wearing a brightly coloured party hat with elasticated chin strap. Carry a balloon and a bottle of wine, and you'll pass off as an innocent party-goer.

F. Fine-Fare, Top Tip, Viz

Eat, Drink and Be Merry ...

As I get older, I'm trying to eat healthy. I've got Gordon Ramsay's new cook book, *Take Two Eggs and Fuck Off.*

Jack Dee

Joan Collins says you are what you eat. She reached this conclusion following experiences in

the swinging sixties and is very careful about
what she puts in her mouth these days.

Mrs Merton

I'm at the age when food has taken the place of
sex in my life. In fact, I've just had a mirror put
over my kitchen table.

Rodney Dangerfield

Gin is a dangerous drink. It's clear and
innocuous looking. You also have to be 45,
female and sitting on the stairs.

Dylan Moran

I'll tell you what I haven't seen for a long time:
my testicles.

John Sparkes

I've gained a few pounds around the middle.
The only lower-body garments I own that still
fit me comfortably are towels.

Dave Barry

I don't have a beer belly. It's a Burgundy belly
and it cost me a lot of money.

Charles Clarke

You can only hold your stomach in for so many
years.

Burt Reynolds

Weighing scales are usually accurate, but never tactful.

Bill Cosby

I had to go to the doctor's last week. He told me to take all my clothes off. Then he said, 'You'll have to diet.' I said, 'What colour?'

Ken Dodd

I'm on a new diet – Viagra and prune juice. I don't know if I'm coming or going.

Rodney Dangerfield

Why is it all the things I like eating have been proven to cause tumours in white mice?

Robert Benchley

Welcome to the Wonderful World of 70: The Oat Bran Years.

Denis Norden

You do live longer with bran, but you spend the last 15 years on the toilet.

Alan King

Life expectancy would grow by leaps and bounds if green vegetables smelled as good as bacon.

Doug Larson

Cabbage she serves me. In ten minutes I could be sky-writing.

Sophia Petrillo, The Golden Girls

I don't eat health foods. At my age I need all the preservative I can get.

George Burns

Age does not diminish the extreme disappointment of having a scoop of ice cream fall from the cone.

Jim Freiberg

Part of the secret of success in life is to eat what you like and let the food fight it out inside.

Mark Twain

Nobody's last words have ever been, 'I wish I'd eaten more rice cakes.'

Amy Krouse Rosenthal

Exercise

You gotta stay in shape. My grandmother started walking 5 miles a day when she was 60. She's 97 today and we don't know where the hell she is.

Ellen DeGeneres

Wrinklies' Wit and Wisdom

I get up at 7am each day to do my exercises –
after I have first put on my make-up. After all, La
Loren is always La Loren.

Sophia Loren, 70

I exercise every morning without fail. Up,
down! Up, down! And then the other eyelid.

Phyllis Diller

I swim a lot. It's either that or buy a new golf
ball.

Bob Hope

I keep fit. Every morning, I do 100 laps of an
Olympic-sized swimming pool – in a small
motor launch.

Peter Cook

Police in Norway stopped Sigrid Krohn de
Lange running down the street in Bergen
because they thought that she had escaped from
a nursing home. The 94-year-old jogger was out
getting fit.

The Irish Independent

My doctor recently told me that jogging could
add years to my life. I think he was right. I feel
10 years older already.

Milton Berle

The only reason I would take up jogging is so I could hear heavy breathing again.

Erma Bombeck

Go jogging? What, and get hit by a meteor?

Robert Benchley

The doctor asked me if I ever got breathless after exercise. I said no, never, because I never exercise.

John Mortimer

I am pushing 60. That is enough exercise for me.

Mark Twain

To get back my youth, I would do anything in the world, except take exercise, get up early, or be respectable.

Oscar Wilde

Whenever I get the urge to exercise, I lie down until the feeling passes away.

Robert M. Hutchins

People are so busy lengthening their lives with exercise that they have no time to live them.

Jonathan Miller

Health nuts are going to feel stupid someday, lying in hospitals dying of nothing.

Redd Foxx

Showbiz and Hollywood

I am in an industry where they eat their elders.

Dale Winton

In Los Angeles, by the time you're 35, you're older than most of the buildings.

Delia Ephron

Actress years seem like dog years and that makes me about 266.

Sharon Stone

I can't think of anything grimmer than being an ageing actress – God! It's worse than being an ageing homosexual.

Candice Bergen

You have to be born a sex symbol. You don't become one. If you're born with it, you'll have it even when you're 100 years old.

Sophia Loren

In Hollywood, great-grandmothers dread
growing old.

Phyllis Batelli

Oscar time is my busiest season. I'm like an
accountant during the tax season.

Richard Fleming, Beverly Hills plastic surgeon

Arnold Schwarzenegger is getting old. He's
changed his catchphrase from 'I'll be back' to
'Oh, my back'.

David Letterman

– You give your age here as 40. I happen to
  know that you are at least 50.
– Oh no, no, no. I absolutely refuse to count the
  last 10 years in Hollywood as part of my life.

Reporter and William Meiklejohn

Adam Faith is only 42, but Terry Nelhams is 62.

Adam Faith

I did not expect an Honorary Oscar – well,
actually, I did. But not for another 25 years.

Federico Fellini

Awards are like haemorrhoids: in the end every
asshole gets one.

Frederic Raphael

That so many people respond to me is fabulous.
It's like having a kind of Alzheimer's disease
where everyone knows you and you don't
know anyone.

Tony Curtis

Hollywood obits are regularly in the high 80s –
these are people who live a long time, which is
what happens if you don't smoke, you work out
every day, you get your body fat awesomely low
and you do only the best cocaine.

David Thomson

Music

The Rolling Stones are on tour again. They
were gonna call the tour 'The Rolling Stones
Live Plus Keith Richards'.

David Letterman

– What do you think John Lennon would have
  been like at 64?
– He would be just John – all that he was
  before. But I think talking about a person's
  age is ageism, like racism or sexism. It isolates
  attitudes.

Yoko Ono

The Rolling Stones are on tour again. They were gonna call the tour 'Hey! You! Get Offa My Stairlift!'

David Letterman

I'm always asked, 'What about being too old to rock 'n' roll?' Presumably lots of writers get better as they get older. So why shouldn't I?

Lou Reed

The Rolling Stones are on tour again. They were gonna call the tour 'And You Thought Aerosmith Was Old'.

David Letterman

I can still rock like a son of a bitch.

Ozzy Osbourne

The Rolling Stones are on tour again. They were gonna call the tour 'We Live Through the Concert or Your Money Back'.

David Letterman

The Grateful Dead are like bad architecture or an old whore. Stick around long enough and you eventually get respectable.

Jerry Garcia

Wrinklies' Wit and Wisdom

The Rolling Stones are on tour again. They were gonna call the tour 'Brown Sugar and Lots of Bran'.

David Letterman

When I give concerts, I ask women not to throw their knickers at me. At my age, I don't want to be a caricature of myself.

Tom Jones

The Rolling Stones are on tour again. They were gonna call the tour 'Under 45s Not Admitted Without a Parent'.

David Letterman

People are always talking about when the Rolling Stones should retire, but it's a racial thing. Nobody ever says B.B. King is too old to play. It's like you can't be white and be an old rock 'n' roller.

David Bailey

The Rolling Stones are on tour again. They were gonna call the tour 'Come Half-Price if You're Mick Jagger's Illegitimate Child'.

David Letterman

Times have changed. Nowadays, when people talk about the stones I want to know if they mean gall or kidney.

Cliff Renwick

The Rolling Stones are on tour again. They were gonna call the tour 'The $140 Million in the Bank Isn't Enough'.

David Letterman

Holding Back the Years

Old Father Time will turn you into a hag if you don't show the bitch who's boss.

Mae West

I don't plan to grow old gracefully. I plan to have face-lifts until my ears meet.

Rita Rudner

I see a lot of new faces. Especially on the old faces.

Johnny Carson

In Los Angeles, people don't get older, they just get tighter.

Greg Proops

I've had so much plastic surgery, if I have one more face-lift it will be a caesarean.

Phyllis Diller

I wish I had a twin, so I could know what I'd look like without plastic surgery.

Joan Rivers

Wrinklies' Wit and Wisdom

Now I'm getting older I take health supplements: geranium, dandelion, passionflower, hibiscus. I feel great, and when I pee, I experience the fresh scent of potpourri.

Sheila Wenz

– I gave Maris botox injections as a gift for our wedding anniversary one year.
– Oh, yes, probably your 10th. That's 'Toxins', isn't it?

Niles and Frasier Crane, Frasier

Moisturisers do work. The rest is pap. There is nothing on God's earth that will take away 30 years of arguing with your husband.

Anita Roddick

Wrinkle cream doesn't work. I've been using it for two years and my balls still look like raisins.

Harland Williams

Anti-wrinkle cream there may be, but anti-fat-bastard cream there is not.

Dave, The Full Monty

The best anti-ageing cream is ice cream. What other food makes you feel like you're 8 years old again?

Anon

Holding Back the Years

The easiest way to diminish the appearance of wrinkles is to keep your glasses off when you look in the mirror.

Joan Rivers

A woman I graduated from college with told me plastic surgery was vulgar, that lines were a sign of character, that it's beautiful to age. I said bull. Character is internal. If you want to present yourself to the world with a face-lift, why the hell not?

Judith Krantz

Everyone in Tinseltown is getting pinched, lifted and pulled. The trade-off is that something of your soul in your face goes away. You end up looking body-snatched.

Robert Redford

I call them the lizard women. They're the ones who have had so much cosmetic surgery that they're no longer biodegradable. They look like giant Komodo dragons with Chanel accessories.

Brett Butler

I wish it were okay in this country to look one's age, whatever it is. Maturity has a lot going for it. For example, you no longer get bubblegum stuck in your brace.

Cyra McFadden

I've not had any surgery. I am too curious to find out exactly how I progress every day of my life naturally. As I've always said, don't fuck around with God.

Elaine Stritch

I love my wife's wrinkles because I know where they come from. Wrinkles are the medals you've won in the battle that is life.

John Peel

How foolish to think that one can ever slam the door in the face of age. Much wiser to be polite and gracious and ask him to lunch in advance.

Noël Coward

To keep the heart unwrinkled, to be hopeful, kindly, cheerful, reverent – that is to triumph over old age.

Thomas Bailey Aldrich

The Fountain of Youth

My recipe for perpetual youth? I've never had my face in the sun, and I have a very handsome young husband ... Sex is one of the best and cheapest beauty treatments there is.

Joan Collins

The Fountain of Youth

The secret of my youthful appearance is simply
– mashed swede. As a face-mask, as a night-cap,
and in an emergency, as a draught-excluder.

Kitty, Victoria Wood

Jewellery takes people's minds off your
wrinkles.

Sonja Henie

Jewellery should be bold. Neat little pearls can
add 10 years.

Joan Collins

If you don't want to get old, don't mellow.

Linda Ellerbee

To have the respect of my peers and the
admiration of young people beats plastic surgery
any day.

Johnny Cash

The fountain of youth is a mixture of gin and
vermouth.

Cole Porter

With them I'm Jack Nicholson. Without them
I'm fat and 60.

Jack Nicholson on his trademark sunglasses

You're only as young as the last time you changed your mind.

Timothy Leary

It's very ageing to talk about age.

Merle Oberon

There is a fountain of youth: it is your mind, your talents, the creativity you bring to your life and to the lives of the people you love.

Sophia Loren

An inordinate passion for pleasure is the secret of remaining young.

Oscar Wilde

People are living longer because of the decline in religion. Not many people believe in the hereafter, so they keep going.

Cyril Clarke

One of the secrets of a long and fruitful life is to forgive everybody everything every night before you go to bed.

Bernard M. Baruch

I have only managed to live so long by carrying no hatreds.

Winston Churchill

The Fountain of Youth

Old people who shine from inside look 10 to 20 years younger.

Dolly Parton

As long as you can still be disappointed, you are still young.

Sarah Churchill

Whatever a man's age, he can reduce it several years by putting a bright-coloured flower in his buttonhole.

Mark Twain

At my age flowers scare me.

George Burns

If you want to stay young-looking, pick your parents very carefully.

Dick Clark

The secret of salvation in old age is this: keep sweet, keep useful, and keep busy.

Elbert Hubbard

The secret to old age: you have to know what you're going to do the next day.

Louis J. Lefkowitz

Wrinklies' Wit and Wisdom

You are young at any age if you are planning for tomorrow. I take inspiration from that wonderful Scottish actor Finlay Currie. Shortly before he died at the age of 90, he was asked on a TV chat show if he'd ever played a romantic lead. 'Not yet, laddie,' he replied. 'Not yet.'

Bob Monkhouse

Humour keeps the elderly rolling along, singing a song. When you laugh, it's an involuntary explosion of the lungs. The lungs need to replenish themselves with oxygen. So you laugh, you breathe, the blood runs, and everything is circulating. If you don't laugh, you'll die.

Mel Brooks

I love to laugh. I think laughter can cure. Either the lines go up or they go down. If they go up, that's a good sign.

Elizabeth Taylor

The heart is the real Fountain of Youth.

Mark Twain

The secret of staying young is to live honestly, eat slowly, and lie about your age.

Lucille Ball

I don't think the trick is staying young. I think the trick is ageing well.

Dr Thomas Perls

We must establish the idea that it is important to look *well*, not to look *young*. It is no more a compliment to say you don't look your age than to say you don't look Jewish or you don't look like an American.

Karen Decrow

– Must you leave so early?
– I must, if I am to keep my youth.
– But why didn't you bring him with you? I should be delighted to meet him.

Lady Cunard and Somerset Maugham

Maturity

You grow up the day you have the first real laugh – at yourself.

Ethel Barrymore

The first sign of maturity is the discovery that the volume knob also turns to the left.

Jerry Wright

You know you've grown up when you become
obsessed with the thermostat.

Jeff Foxworthy

What I look forward to is continued
immaturity followed by death.

Dave Barry

Age is a very high price to pay for maturity.

Tom Stoppard

Tony Benn immatures with age.

Harold Wilson

No one is ever old enough to know better.

Holbrook Jackson

When I grow up I want to be a little boy.

Joseph Heller

A person's maturity consists in having found
again the seriousness one had as a child at play.

Friedrich Wilhelm Nietzsche

Act Your Age

The older you get, the more important it is not
to act your age.

Ashleigh Brilliant

We don't stop playing because we grow old, we grow old because we stop playing.

George Bernard Shaw

I've always believed the secret of eternal youth is arrested development.

Alice Roosevelt Longworth

The ageing process has you firmly in its grasp if you never get the urge to throw a snowball.

Doug Larson

Even though I'm very old, I always feel like the youngest person in the room.

W.H. Auden

To be young, really young, takes a very long time.

Pablo Picasso

The secret of genius is to carry the spirit of the child into old age, which means never losing your enthusiasm.

Aldous Huxley

The great man is one who never loses his child's heart.

Mencius

I have the heart of a small child. I keep it in a jar on my desk.

Stephen King

I'm Not Menthyl

MALAPROPISMS

My nan, God bless 'er, gets things a bit mixed up. She said to me the other day, 'I've bought one of those new George Formby grills.'

Peter Kay

– Barbara, didn't Elsie next door have implants?
– No, eggplants, Mam.

Nana and Barbara Royle, The Royle Family

My mother thinks a crouton's a Japanese sofa.

Mary Unfaithful

– He's autistic, Gran.
– That's nice. I wish I could draw.

Martin and Millicent Smith

Our Susan's still not had her baby. If she doesn't have it soon she'll have to be seduced.

Brenda Sneddon

Mark my words: her chickens will come home to roast.

Coral Greene

My mum said, 'I saw whatsaname last week, oh, whatshisname, I can never remember anything these days – it's this damned anorexia.'

Stephen Fry

I can't be doin' with Donny Osmond and that bunch of Morons.

Bert Fletcher

My nan was complaining of chest pains. I said, 'Are you all right, Nan?' She said, 'I think I've got vagina.'

Peter Kay

Oh, love, can you get me some of that cunnilinctus for my cough?

Edna Steele

I've got bigger fish to fly!

Elsie Mason

The patio doors are sticking again. Have you got some of that UB40?

Phyllis Amison

The doctor says I have to have a hearing aid because there's a blockage in my Euston station tube.

Joe Hadley

I don't want to see a pieciatrist; I'm not menthyl!

Hylda Baker, Nearest and Dearest

I don't want to end up in an old folk's home wearing incompetence pads. I'm still compost mentis.

Harriet Wynn

An elderly lady came into the chemist and asked for a bottle of euthanasia. I didn't say anything. I just handed her a bottle of echinacea.

Lydia Berryman

Money

When I was young, I thought money was the most important thing in life. Now that I'm old, I know it is.

Oscar Wilde

Don't grow old without money, honey.

Lena Horne

If you're given the choice between money and sex appeal, take the money. As you get older, the money will become your sex appeal.

Katharine Hepburn

Three things have helped me successfully through the ordeals of life: an understanding husband, a good analyst, and millions of dollars.

Mary Tyler Moore

If you think nobody cares whether you are alive or dead, try missing a couple of car payments.

Ann Landers

I have enough money to last me the rest of my life – unless I have to buy something.

Jackie Mason

There are no luggage-racks on hearses, no pockets in shrouds.

Anon

Pleasures and Perks of Growing Older

As you grow old, you lose interest in sex, your friends drift away, and your children often ignore you. There are other advantages, of course, but these are the outstanding ones.

Richard Needham

Wrinklies' Wit and Wisdom

– You know the best thing about being old?
– Cardigans?
– No. Disabled parking spaces.

Anon

One compensation of old age is that it excuses you from picnics.

William Feather

One of the delights of being a senior citizen is it's easy to annoy young people. Step 1: get in the car. Step 2: turn the indicator on. Step 3: leave it on for 50 miles.

David Letterman

I can't wait to get old enough to ride in one of those buggies at the airport. Whizzing past all those poor sods on the long trek to the departure gate. It will make being old worthwhile.

Sean Needham

One good thing about being old and having a failing memory is that I can enjoy the endless repeats of programmes like *Inspector Morse*, *Murder She Wrote*, and *Midsomer Murders* because I can never remember whodunit.

Larry Simpkins

Pleasures and Perks of Growing Older

One of the good things about getting older is that you find you're more interesting than most of the people you meet.

Lee Marvin

I basically enjoy getting older because I get smarter. So what I have to say is more worth listening to, in my opinion.

Clive James

I used to dread getting older because I thought I would not be able to do all the things I wanted to do, but now that I am older I find that I don't want to do them.

Nancy Astor, 80

One of the delights known to age, and beyond the grasp of youth, is that of Not Going.

J.B. Priestley

By the bye, as I must leave off being young, I find many Douceurs in being a sort of Chaperon for I am put on the Sofa near the fire & can drink as much wine as I like.

Jane Austen

My husband's idea of a good night out is a good night in.

Maureen Lipman

Wrinklies' Wit and Wisdom

I think happiness is easier to come by when you're older: Go for a nice walk and do some push-ups. Sex is always good. A hamburger will work, if you make it right and make it yourself. It should be rare and have raw onion and a lot of mustard. A martini, just one, is really fabulous. Going to Mass on Sunday morning, if it is the right sort of Mass, when the homily is short and the choir hangs together just right … Sleep. Sleep is always good. You almost always feel better when you wake up. Baseball games. And Louis Armstrong …

Garrison Keillor

One of the many pleasures of old age is giving things up.

Malcolm Muggeridge

I always make a point of starting the day at 6am with champagne. It goes straight to the heart and cheers one up. White wine won't do. You need the bubbles.

John Mortimer

Pottering is the most fun you can have in slippers.

Guy Browning

Pleasures and Perks of Growing Older

I am getting to an age when I can only enjoy
the last sport left. It is called hunting for your
spectacles.

Lord Grey of Falloden

The great thing about being in your 70s is, what
can they do to you? What have you got to lose?
Freedom is just another word for having
nothing left to lose.

Clint Eastwood

As a man grows older it is harder and harder to
frighten him.

Jean Paul Richter

All one's life as a young woman one is on show,
people notice you. You set yourself up to be
noticed and admired. And then, not expecting
it, you become middle aged and anonymous.
No one notices you. You achieve a wonderful
freedom. It is a positive thing. You can move
about, unnoticed and invisible.

Doris Lessing

Bored? Here's a way the over-50 set can easily kill
a good half hour: 1) Place your car keys in your
right hand. 2) With your left hand call a friend
and confirm a lunch or dinner date. 3) Hang up
the phone. 4) Now look for your car keys.

Steve Martin

Now I'm getting older, I don't need to do drugs anymore. I can get the same effect just by standing up real fast.

Jonathan Katz

If I'm feeling really wild I don't bother flossing before bedtime.

Judith Viorst

My kitchen linoleum is so black and shiny that I waltz while I wait for the kettle to boil. This pleasure is for the old who live alone.

Florida Scott-Maxwell

A few perks of old age: things I buy now won't wear out; I enjoy hearing arguments about pensions; my secrets are safe with my friends because they can't remember them either.

Felicity Muir

There's nothing like a flutter on the horses for a bit of excitement. Might raise the blood pressure but not as threatening as nicotine and alcohol.

Dorothy Norton

The nice thing about being old is that it doesn't affect your betting; in fact, old people betting makes more sense than young people betting.

Pleasures and Perks of Growing Older

The lady in the bookie's said to me, 'Do you like having a little bet?' I told her no, I loathed it. I like to make *big* bets.

Clement Freud

One of my pleasures is to read in bed every night a few pages of P.G. Wodehouse, so that if I die in my sleep it will be with a smile on my face.

Arthur Marshall

One of the advantages of being 70 is that you need only 4 hours' sleep. True, you need it 4 times a day, but still.

Denis Norden

One good thing about getting older is that if you're getting married, the phrase 'till death do you part' doesn't sound so horrible. It only means about 10 or 15 years and not the eternity it used to mean.

Joy Behar

One of the greatest pleasures of growing old is looking back at the people you didn't marry.

Elizabeth Taylor

One of the pleasures of age is to *find out* that one *was* right, and that one was much righter than one knew at say 17 or 23.

Ezra Pound

Wrinklies' Wit and Wisdom

The joy of being older is that in one's life one can, towards the end of the run, overact appallingly.

Quentin Crisp

Given 3 requisites – means of existence, reasonable health, and an absorbing interest – those years beyond 60 can be the happiest and most satisfying of a lifetime.

Earnest Calkins

Is not old wine wholesomest, old pippins toothsomest, old wood burns brightest, old linen wash whitest, and old lovers soundest?

John Webster

At 60 a man has passed most of the reefs and whirlpools. Excepting death, he has no enemies left to meet. That man has awakened to a new youth. He is young.

George Luks

We grow not older with years, but newer every day.

Emily Dickinson

The older you get, the better you get – unless you're a banana.

Anon

Pleasures and Perks of Growing Older

One positive thing about getting older is that you develop a sense of perspective about your legacy to future generations. People say things like, 'We're going to use up our Earth's resources. The Earth will be uninhabitable by 2050.' And I find myself nodding and going, 'No problem, I'll be dead.'

Dave Barry

As I move, graciously I hope, toward the door marked Exit, it occurs to me that the only thing I ever really liked to do was go to the movies.

Gore Vidal

Did you know that by the time he'd turned 80, Winston Churchill had coronary thrombosis, 3 attacks of pneumonia, a hernia, 2 strokes and something known as a senile itch? All the same, though often setting fire to himself, he still managed to enjoy a cigar.

Beryl Bainbridge

I smoke 10 to 15 cigars a day. At my age, if I don't have something to hang on to, I'll fall over.

George Burns

At the age of 80, there are very few pleasures left to me, but one of them is passive smoking.

Baroness Trumpington

– You're 86 years old. You smoke 10 cigars a day,
  drink 5 martinis a day, surround yourself with
  beautiful women. What does your doctor say
  about all this?
– My doctor is dead.

Interviewer and George Burns

If you resolve to give up smoking, drinking and
loving, you don't actually live longer – it just
seems longer.

Clement Freud

No pleasure is worth giving up for the sake of
two more years in a geriatric home in Weston-
super-Mare.

Kingsley Amis

The toll of time brings few delights in facing
age's deadly spike; atop the list perhaps is this:
outliving those we didn't like.

Art Buck

There's one advantage to being 102. No peer
pressure.

Dennis Wolfberg

I feel very old sometimes. I carry on and would
not like to die before having emptied a few

more buckets of shit on the heads of my fellow men.

Gustave Flaubert

I advise you to go on living solely to enrage those who are paying your annuities. It is the only pleasure I have left. When I feel an attack of indigestion coming on, I picture two or three princes as gainers by my death, take courage out of spite, and conspire against them with rhubarb and temperance.

Voltaire

The older one grows, the more one likes indecency.

Virginia Woolf

I've got cheekier with age. You can get away with murder when you're 71 years old. People just think I'm a silly old fool.

Bernard Manning

At 50, the madwoman in the attic breaks loose, stomps down the stairs, and sets fire to the house. She won't be imprisoned anymore.

Erica Jong

Women may be the one group that grows more radical with age.

Gloria Steinem

Wrinklies' Wit and Wisdom

I know I'm going to get old and be one of those crazy women who sits on balconies and spits on people and screams, 'Get a haircut!'

Carrie Fisher

Everything got better after I was 50. I wrote my best books. I walked Pillar, starting from Buttermere, which I'm told no fell walker of advanced years should attempt.

A.J.P. Taylor

I sometimes think that God will ask us, 'That wonderful world of mine, why didn't you enjoy it more?'

Ronald Blythe

Good days are to be gathered like sunshine in grapes, to be trodden and bottled into wine and kept for age to sip at ease beside the fire. If the traveller has vintaged well, he need trouble to wander no longer; the ruby moments glow in his glass at will.

Freya Stark

Look at everything as though you were seeing it either for the first or last time. Then your time on earth will be filled with glory.

Betty Smith

The birds sing louder when you grow old.

Rose Chernin

Pleasures and Perks of Growing Older

When it is dark enough, you can see the stars.

Charles A. Beard

I am spending delightful afternoons in my garden, watching everything living around me. As I grow older, I feel everything departing, and I love everything with more passion.

Emile Zola

The happiness of finding idleness a duty. No more opinions, no more politics, no more practical tasks.

W.B. Yeats

Sometimes it's fun to sit in your garden and try to remember your dog's name.

Steve Martin

I've always thought that very few people grow old as admirably as academics. At least books never let them down.

Margaret Drabble

A truly great book should be read in youth, again in maturity and once more in old age, as a fine building should be seen by morning light, at noon and by moonlight.

Robertson Davies

Old books that have ceased to be of service should no more be abandoned than should old friends who have ceased to give pleasure.

Bernard M. Baruch

At 76, there is nothing nicer than nodding off while reading. Going fast asleep then being woken up by the crash of the book on the floor, then saying to myself, well it doesn't matter much. An admirable feeling.

A.J.P. Taylor

Think what a better world it would be if we all, the whole world, had cookies and milk about 3 o'clock every afternoon and then lay down on our blankets for a nap.

Barbara Jordan

A nap in the middle of the day can do you good. If you wake up in your pyjamas – it's morning. If you're in your clothes – it's time for tea.

Thora Hird

I'm getting on. I'm now equipped with a snooze button.

Denis Norden

In spite of illness, in spite even of the arch-enemy sorrow, one can remain alive long past the usual date of disintegration if one is unafraid of change, insatiable in intellectual curiosity, interested in big things, and happy in small ways.

Edith Wharton

The woman who has a gift for old age is the woman who delights in comfort. If warmth is known as the blessing it is, if your bed, your bath, your best-liked food and drink are regarded as fresh delights, then you know how to thrive when old.

Florida Scott-Maxwell

Happiness in the older years of life, like happiness in every year of life, is a matter of choice – *your* choice for yourself. Happiness is to trim the day to one's own mood and feeling, to raise the window shade of your own bedroom an hour early and squander the hour in the morning sunshine, to drink your own tea from your own teacup, to practise the little wisdoms of housekeeping, to hang a picture on the wall where memories can reach out to it a dozen times a day and to sit in your kitchen and talk to your friend.

Harold Azine

Wrinklies' Wit and Wisdom

I try to make each day a miniature lifetime in which I achieve something and I enjoy something.

Leslie Bricusse

If I had known when I was 21 that I should be as happy as I am now, at 70, I should have been sincerely shocked. They promised me wormwood and funeral raven.

Christopher Isherwood

Happiness in old age is, more than anything else, preserving the privileges of privacy.

Harold Azine

During much of my life, I was anxious to be what someone else wanted me to be. Now I have given up that struggle. I am what I am.

Elizabeth Coatsworth

I love having the freedom to do what I want, when I want and not care a darn what anyone else thinks. Like the old lady in Jenny Jones' poem, 'I shall spend my pension on brandy and summer gloves,' and no one can stop me!

Lilian Howard

One pleasure attached to growing older is that many things seem to be growing younger;

growing fresher and more lively than we once supposed them to be.

G.K. Chesterton

The great thing about getting older is that you don't lose all the other ages you've been.

Madeleine L'Engle

From 51 to 53 I have been happy, and would like to remind others that their turn can come too. It is the only message worth giving.

E.M. Forster

Let us cherish and enjoy old age; for it is full of pleasure, if you know how to use it. Fruit tastes most delicious just when its season is ending.

Seneca

Pick More Daisies

REGRETS

– You're now 76 years old. Do you have any regrets in life?
– Yes, I haven't had enough sex.

Interviewer and John Betjeman

Wrinklies' Wit and Wisdom

My one regret in life is that I am not someone else.

Woody Allen

My greatest regret is not knowing at 30 what I knew about women at 60.

Arthur Miller

I rather regret I haven't taken more drugs. Is it too late, at 70, to try cocaine? Would it be dangerous or interesting?

Joan Bakewell

If I had my life to live over again, I'd make the same mistakes – only sooner.

Tallulah Bankhead

You know, by the time you reach my age, you've made plenty of mistakes if you've lived your life properly.

Ronald Reagan, 76

The only thing in my life that I regret is that I once saved David Frost from drowning. I had to pull him out, otherwise nobody would have believed I didn't push him in.

Peter Cook

My only regret in life is that I did not drink more champagne.

John Maynard Keynes

If I had my life to live over again, I would do everything the exact same way, with the possible exception of seeing the movie remake of *Lost Horizon*.

Woody Allen

If I had my life to live over, I would pick more daisies.

Nadine Stair

If I had it all to do over again, I would spend more time with my children. I would make my money before spending it. I would learn the joys of wine instead of hard liquor. I would not smoke cigarettes when I had pneumonia. I would not marry the fifth time.

John Huston

If I had my life to live over, I'd live over a saloon.

W.C. Fields

If I had to live my life over again, I'd be a plumber.

Albert Einstein

Wrinklies' Wit and Wisdom

If I had my life to live over, I don't think I'd have the strength.

Flip Wilson

If I had my life to live over again, I would have cried and laughed less while watching television and more while watching life. I would have sat on the lawn with my children and not worried about grass stains. When my kids kissed me impetuously, I would not have said, 'Later. Now go get washed for dinner.' There would have been more I love yous and more I'm sorries. I would seize every minute ... look at it and really see it ... live it ... and never give it back.

Erma Bombeck

I regret having been so polite in the past. I'd like to trample on at least a dozen people.

Harold Brodkey

If I have my life to live over again I should form the habit of nightly composing myself to thoughts of death. There is no other practice which so intensifies life.

Muriel Spark

Looking back, I have this to regret, that too often when I loved, I did not say so.

David Grayson

The trouble with reaching the age of 92 is that
regrets for a misspent life are bound to creep in,
and whenever you see me with a furrowed
brow you can be sure that what is on my mind
is the thought that if only I had taken up golf
earlier and devoted my whole time to it instead
of fooling about writing stories and things, I
might have got my handicap down to under 18.

P.G. Wodehouse

As you grow older, you'll find the only things
you regret are the things you didn't do.

Zachary Scott

A man is not old until regrets take the place of
your dreams.

John Barrymore

I've never really learnt how to live, and I've
discovered too late that life is for living.

John Reith

Never regret. If it's good, it's wonderful. It it's
bad, it's experience.

Victoria Holt

Maybe all one can do is hope to end up with
the right regrets.

Arthur Miller

If I Knew Then What I Know Now — So What?
                    Estelle Getty, title of her autobiography

Mustn't Grumble?

I was brought up to respect my elders and now I'm 87 I don't have to respect *anybody*.

                              George Burns

Been There, Done That, Don't Give a F★★★
What Anybody Thinks Anymore

                    Slogan on a senior citizen's T-shirt

I wish I loved the Human Race;
I wish I loved its silly face;
I wish I liked the way it walks;
I wish I liked the way it talks;
And when I'm introduced to one
I wish I thought What Jolly fun!

  Walter Alexander Raleigh, Wishes of an Elderly Man

At age 20, we worry about what others think of us; at 40, we don't care what they think of us; at 60, we discover they haven't been thinking of us at all.

                              Bob Hope

I don't want a flu jab. I like getting flu. It gives me something else to complain about.

David Letterman

There's no law that decrees when and when not to whinge, but you reach a certain age – 80 seems about right – when you're expected to manifest querulousness – the coffee's too hot, the boiled egg's too soft …

Clement Freud

Bloody birthdays. Bloody women. Bloody everything. Bloody hell … Bloody footmark on the carpet now. Bloody people coming in with wet shoes …

Victor Meldrew, One Foot in the Grave

Three milk stouts – and make sure there's no lipstick on the glasses.

Ena Sharples, Coronation Street

Edith Evans bought an incredibly expensive Renoir and, when a friend asked her why she had hung it so low on the wall, out of the light behind the curtain, she replied curtly, 'Because there was a hook.'

Stephen Fry

Wrinklies' Wit and Wisdom

Just because I'm in a wheelchair they think they can push me around … I coped when a bull mastiff tried to mate with my left-side tyre.

Maud Grimes, Coronation Street

Senior Citizen: Give me my Damn Discount

Slogan on a senior citizen's T-shirt

When I was young I was frightened I might bore people. Now I'm old I am frightened they will bore me.

Ruth Adam

Many older people are not sweet old things asking for a seat on the bus; they are in many cases demanding a turn in the driver's seat.

Michael Simmons

I'm Ageing With Attitude. I am the future. We will not be crumbling ruins.

Janet Street-Porter

The Devil's in her tongue, and so 'tis in most women's of her age; for when it has quitted the tail, it repairs to the upper tier.

Aphra Behn

May your shampoo get mixed up with your
Preparation H and shrink your head to the size
of a mushroom.

Anon

Nobody hears old people complain because
people think that's all old people do. And that's
because old people are gnarled and sagged and
twisted into the shape of a complaint.

Edward Albee

I refused to go on that *Grumpy Old Men*
programme because I said, 'If I go on, I will be
grumpy about grumpy old men.'

Stephen Fry

Sometimes I wake up grumpy; other times I let
him sleep.

Car bumper sticker

I'm 101 years old and at my age, honey, I can say
what I want!

Bessie Delany

Menopause

*Is It Me Or Is It Hot in Here? A Realistic Guide to
The Menopause*

Jenni Murray, book title

Wrinklies' Wit and Wisdom

The menopause is the stage that woman goes through when her body, through a complex biological process, senses that the woman has reached the stage in her life where her furniture is much too nice for her to have a baby barfing on it.

Dave Barry

– Oh my God, Saffy, darling, help. I'm having a hot flush. I don't believe it. It's a hot flush. Feel my skin.
– Mum, you're standing too close to the kettle.

Edina and Saffron Monsoon, Absolutely Fabulous

Someone told me that giving up chocolate would reduce my hot flushes. To be honest, I prefer the hot flushes.

Anna Granger

I like the hot flushes. It's like being in love again without the aggravation.

Joy Behar

Real women don't have hot flushes, they have power surges.

Car bumper sticker

It's the menopause. I've got my own climate.

Julie Walters

Menopause

I went to see my doctor to talk to him about this menopause thing, because I don't know if I really want to do it.

Jane Condon

A friend of mine, Norma Cowles, started The Change at Pontins in Torquay but there were absolutely no menopausal facilities there whatsoever. Something for Judith Chalmers to think about.

Mrs Merton

My grandma told me, 'The good news is, after menopause the hair on your legs gets really thin and you don't have to shave anymore. Which is great because it means you have more time to work on your new moustache.'

Karen Haber

I refuse to think of them as chin hairs. I think of them as stray eyebrows.

Janette Barber

I'm trying very hard to understand the younger generation. They have adjusted the timetable for childbearing so that menopause and teaching a 16-year-old how to drive a car will occur in the same week.

Erma Bombeck

Why did the menopausal woman cross the road? To kill the chicken.

Jane Condon

At Least I Have My Health

I've just become a pensioner so I've started saving up for my own hospital trolley.

Tom Baker

The time will come in your life, it will almost certainly come, when the voice of God will thunder at you from a cloud, 'From this day forth thou shalt not be able to put on thine own socks.'

John Mortimer

I feel age like an icicle down my back.

Dyson Carter

When I wake up in the morning and nothing hurts, I know I must be dead.

George Burns

I don't need you to remind me of my age, I have a bladder to do that for me.

Stephen Fry

At Least I Have My Health

When you get to my age, life seems little more than one long march to and from the lavatory.

John Mortimer

At 75, I sleep like a log. I never have to get up in the middle of the night to go to the bathroom. I go in the morning. Every morning, like clockwork, at 7am, I pee. Unfortunately, I don't wake up till 8.

Harry Beckworth

Thanks to modern medical advances such as antibiotics, nasal spray and Diet Coke, it has become routine for people in the civilized world to pass the age of 40, sometimes more than once.

Dave Barry

When I was 40, my doctor advised me that a man in his 40s shouldn't play tennis. I heeded his advice carefully and could hardly wait until I reached 50 to start again.

Hugo Black

When I turned 50, I went off to have my prostate checked because I kept reading I should. Fucking finger up the arse, I can do without that again.

Bob Geldof

Wrinklies' Wit and Wisdom

Be suspicious of any doctor who tries to take your temperature with his finger.

David Letterman

– How do you know which pills to take?
– Doesn't make any difference. Whatever they fix, I got.

Oscar Madison and Felix Ungar, The Odd Couple II

My mother is no spring chicken, although she has got as many chemicals in her as one.

Dame Edna Everage

Why do the medical profession still keep writing on prescription bottles in a size that only a 20-year-old can read? You were standing there with the medicine bottle in your hand and you died because you couldn't read the directions.

Bill Cosby

Half the modern drugs could well be thrown out the window, except that the birds might eat them.

Martin H. Fischer

I don't know much about medicine, but I know what I like.

S.J. Perelman

At Least I Have My Health

Casey came home from seeing the doctor looking very worried. His wife said, 'What's the problem?' He said, 'The doctor told me I have to take a pill every day for the rest of my life.' She said, 'So what, lots of people have to take a pill every day for the rest of their lives.' He said, 'I know, but he only gave me four.'

Hal Roach

The good Lord never gives you more than you can handle. Unless you die of something.

Steve Martin

You're 50 years old! Can they make a drug to help you through all of that, to keep all your organs intact until your golden years? No. Can they make a drug to give mental clarity to your golden time? No. What they've got is Viagra, a drug to make you harder than Chinese algebra.

Robin Williams

The doctor said, 'I have good news and bad news. The good news is: you're not a hypochondriac.'

Bob Monkhouse

The doctor said to me, 'You're going to live till you're 60.' I said, 'I am 60.' He said, 'What did I tell you?'

Henny Youngman

Wrinklies' Wit and Wisdom

When you get to my age, getting a second doctor's opinion is like switching slot machines.

James Walker

Now I'm over 50 my doctor says I should go out and get more fresh air and exercise. I said, 'All right, I'll drive with the car window open.'

Angus Walker

How can people complain about the length of time spent waiting in Out Patients for an appointment? I've spent many happy hours in our local hospital familiarizing myself with people's ailments and afflictions.

Mrs Merton

Whoever thought up the word 'Mammogram'? Every time I hear it, I think I'm supposed to put my breast in an envelope and send it to someone.

Jan King

Everyone goes into an aeroplane or a hospital wondering if they'll ever get out of either alive.

Richard Gordon

I was under the care of a couple of medical students who couldn't diagnose a decapitation.

Jeffrey Bernard

There's nothing wrong with you that an expensive operation can't prolong.

Graham Chapman

The NHS don't think of it as having lost a patient, more as having gained a bed.

Anon

He's on the mend, sitting up in bed blowing the froth off his medicine.

Flann O'Brien

Getting out of the hospital is a lot like resigning from a book club. You're not out of it until the computer says you're out of it.

Erma Bombeck

I rang the Enema Helpline. They were very rude.

Jack Dee

Always keep tubes of haemorrhoid ointment and Deep Heat rub well separated in your bathroom cabinet.

P. Turner, Top Tip, Viz

I'm at an age where my back goes out more than I do.

Phyllis Diller

Wrinklies' Wit and Wisdom

No one should grow old who isn't ready to appear ridiculous.

John Mortimer

You don't know real embarrassment until your hip sets off a metal detector.

Ross McGuiness

One of the most embarrassing moments when you get to my age is to have to urinate under pressure with a line behind you. I step up to the urinal full of dreams of instant relief, only to find my body saying, *Why are we here?*

Bill Cosby

1960s Versus 1990s …

Then: getting into a new hip joint
Now: getting a new hip joint

Then: long hair
Now: longing for hair

Then: killer weed
Now: weed killer

Then: taking acid
Now: taking antacid

At Least I Have My Health

Then: trying to look like Elizabeth Taylor
Now: trying not to look like Elizabeth Taylor

Anon

Growing old brings some disadvantages, like
you start having trouble with the coconut ones
in Liquorice Allsorts; bending over becomes a
major decision; and you can't count the
number of times a day you find yourself
moving in one direction when you should be
moving in the other.

Denis Norden

Of all the self-fulfilling prophecies in our
culture, the assumption that ageing means
decline and poor health is probably the
deadliest.

Marilyn Ferguson

Age is a product of good health. Our research
shows that people who live to be 100 are as
mentally and physically healthy as people 30
years younger. We've replaced the saying, 'The
older you get, the sicker you get,' with the
more accurate, 'The older you get, the
healthier you've been.'

Dr Thomas Perls

Wrinklies' Wit and Wisdom

There are many mysteries in old age but the greatest, surely, is this: in those adverts for walk-in bathtubs, why doesn't all the water gush out when you get in?

Alan Coren

Have you seen the afternoon telly they put on for poor old crocks and old-age-perishers? You're just dozing off to a black and white film starring James Mason when he was in short trousers, when on comes that chap from *All Creatures Great and Small* saying, 'Have you thought about your funeral?' Then on comes some old girl whizzing up and down stairs on a stairlift. It's all based on fear and meant to scare you.

Ken Dodd

We have put more effort into helping folks reach old age than into helping them enjoy it.

Frank A. Clark

My wife's aunt is about 109 years old and has a pair of glasses for every activity you can imagine – glasses for knitting, glasses for reading, glasses for doing the crossword. But she's always losing them. 'Have you seen my glasses?' she'll say. 'Surely you have a pair of looking-for-your-glasses glasses, don't you?'

Jack Dee

It's extraordinary. My mother doesn't need glasses at all and here I am 52, 56 – well, whatever age I am – and can't see a thing.

Queen Elizabeth II

My grandmother is over 80 and still doesn't need glasses. Drinks right out of the bottle.

Henny Youngman

I prefer to forget both pairs of glasses and pass my declining years saluting strange women and grandfather clocks.

Ogden Nash

From the age of 75 on, I have found my memory deteriorating and my senses getting less acute. I can mistake a reference to 'Stena Sealink' on television for 'Denis Healey'.

Denis Healey

My dad became more and more deaf, relying on lip-reading to understand people, and almost to spite him, my mother became a Moslem Fundamentalist.

Harry Hill

Wrinklies' Wit and Wisdom

My granny wore a hearing aid that was always tuned too low. Because when she turned it up, it whistled, and every dog in Dublin rushed to her side.

Terry Wogan

When I turn my hearing aid up to 10, I can hear a canary break wind 6 miles away.

Sophia Petrillo, The Golden Girls

My grandmother was insane. She had pierced hearing aids.

Steven Wright

I had a job selling hearing aids door to door. It wasn't easy, because your best prospects never answered.

Bob Monkhouse

It's been said that if you're not radical at 20, you have no heart; if you're still radical at 40, you have no brain. Of course, either way, at 60 you usually have no teeth.

Bill Maher

– Dorothy, have you seen my teeth?
– They're in your mouth, Ma.

– I know that. Don't they look good today, I
ran them through the dishwasher.

Sophia Petrillo and Dorothy Zbornak, The Golden Girls

My 92-year-old aunt, in hospital to have a
pacemaker fitted, was asked by the nurse
preparing her for the operation: 'Please give me
your teeth.' 'Certainly not,' was her stern reply.
She still has her own.

Roger Lines

I visited a new dentist for my 6-monthly check-up.
Having given me the all clear, he glanced at my
notes, then remarked: 'Those should see you out.'

Angela Walder, 72

From the bathroom came the sound of my
grandmother brushing her tooth.

Peter de Vries

My father kept several pairs of false teeth, one
set in a jar marked 'Best Pair', another marked
'Next Best' and a third marked 'Not Bad'.

David Hockney

My friend, George, has false teeth – with braces
on them.

Steven Wright

When you're my age, you just never risk being
ill – because then everyone says, 'Oh, he's done
for.'

John Gielgud

You will die not because you are ill. You will die
because you are alive.

Seneca

Never talk about yourself as being *old*. There *is*
something in Mind Cure, after all, and, if you
continually talk of yourself as being old, you
may perhaps bring on some of the infirmities of
age.

Hannah Smith

No one sophisticated, glamorous or interesting
over 60 talks about age. So why then do other
people react to life after 60 as though it were a
sludge-coloured blanket which they've pulled
defiantly around them crocheted large with the
word 'OLD'?

Marcelle D'Argy-Smith

Old age means a crown of thorns, and the trick
is to wear it jauntily.

Christopher Morley

Eighty years old! No eyes left, no ears, no teeth, no legs, no wind! And when all is said and done, how astonishingly well one does without them!

Paul Claudel

Use your health, even to the point of wearing it out. That is what it is for. Spend all you have before you die; do not outlive yourself.

George Bernard Shaw

I'm not to blame for an old body, but I would be to blame for an old soul. An old soul is a shameful thing.

Margaret Deland

No Medical, and No Salesman Will Call

INSURANCE

What would make life better for old people? Axe that Churchill Insurance 'nodding dog' commercial on television.

Clement Freud

All big stars of my parents' generation are on Cable TV selling things. Insurance policies to the elderly, asking them to send in $7.95 out of their last 8 dollars for a policy that will leave money to children who don't visit them.

Louie Anderson

Life insurance is a weird concept. You really don't get anything for it. It works like this: you pay me money and when you die, I'll pay you money.

Bill Kirchenbauer

There are worse things in life than death. Have you ever spent an evening with an insurance salesman?

Woody Allen

I detest life insurance agents; they always argue that I shall some day die, which is not so.

Stephen Leacock

I took a physical for some life insurance. All they would give me was fire and theft.

Milton Berle

I have done many insurance physical check-ups on people and as far as I can tell, an insurance physical can only determine one thing –

whether or not you are going to die during the
physical.

Dr Mark DePaolis

My wife and I took out life insurance policies
on one another, so now it's just a waiting game.

Bill Dwyer

Going Gaga

They say that after the age of 20 you lose
50,000 brain cells a day. I don't believe it. I think
it's much more.

Ned Sherrin

A 'senior moment' is a euphemism to indicate a
temporary loss of marbles to anyone over 50.

Anon

As you get older, you've probably noticed that
you tend to forget things. You'll be talking at a
party, and you'll *know* that you know this
person, but no matter how hard you try, you
can't remember his or her name. This can be
very embarrassing, especially if he or she turns
out to be your spouse.

Dave Barry

Wrinklies' Wit and Wisdom

Remembering something at first try is now as good as an orgasm as far as I'm concerned.

Gloria Steinem

First, you forget names, then you forget faces. Next, you forget to pull your zipper up and finally you forget to pull it down.

Leo Rosenberg

My memory's starting to go. The only thing I still retain is water.

Alex Cole

To my deafness I'm accustomed,
To my dentures I'm resigned,
I can manage my bifocals,
But O, how I miss my mind.

Anon

– Hurry up, Dorothy, we're going to be late for Temple.
– Ma, it's Tuesday and we're Catholic.

Sophia Petrillo and Dorothy Zbornak, The Golden Girls

'You are old, Father William,' the young man said,
'And your hair has become very white;
And yet you incessantly stand on your head –
Do you think, at your age, it is right?'

'In my youth,' Father William replied to
   his son,
'I feared it might injure the brain;
But, now that I'm perfectly sure I have
   none,
Why, I do it again and again.'

Lewis Carroll

I had always looked on myself as a sort of freak
whom age could not touch, which was where I
made the ruddy error, because I'm really a senile
wreck with about one and a half feet in the grave.

P.G. Wodehouse, 69

His golf bag doesn't contain a full set of irons.

Robin Williams

I still have a full deck. I just shuffle slower.

Milton Berle

Spare a thought for my friend Eliza Hamilton,
who was wrongly diagnosed as mentally
unstable when all she was was a bit giddy.

Mrs Merton

The Mayoress was visiting an old folk's home.
As she went round she saw an old lady sitting
there, and said to her, brightly, 'Good
morning.' The old lady looked a bit puzzled,

so the Mayoress said, 'Do you know who I am?' The old lady gave her a sympathetic look and said, 'No, dear, but if you ask the matron, she'll tell you.'

Anon

Been There, Done That, Can't Remember.

Slogan on a senior citizen's T-shirt

– Can you remember any of your past lives?
– At my age I have a problem remembering what happened yesterday.

Interviewer and the Dalai Lama

The face is familiar, but I can't remember my name.

Robert Benchley

At my age, you learn a new name, you gotta forget an old one.

Wesley Birdsong, Lone Star

That phrase they use, 'in living memory' – as in 'the worst floods in living memory' or 'the coldest winter in living memory' – just how far back does it stretch because at my age my 'living memory' goes back to a week last Tuesday.

Alan Coren

I remember things that happened 60 years ago, but if you ask me where I left my car keys five minutes ago, that's sometimes a problem.

Lou Thesz

When I was younger I could remember anything, whether it happened or not, but I am getting old and now that I am 71 I shall soon remember only the latter.

Mark Twain

All the failures of memory that can plague you, such as losing your car at the mall or losing your glasses on your forehead or losing the reason you entered a room, are minor when compared to the most embarrassing trick your mind can play: forgetting what you've been talking about. How come I can remember events of 30 years ago but not what I said in the last 30 seconds.

Bill Cosby

I know a lot of old people. They're all the same. They're cranky. They're demanding. They repeat themselves. They're cranky.

Sophia Petrillo, The Golden Girls

They *will* all have heard that story of yours before – but if you tell it *well* they won't mind hearing it again.

Thora Hird

My grandmother's 85 and starting to get forgetful. The family's upset about it but I don't mind because I get 8 cheques on my birthday from her. That's 40 bucks.

Tom Arnold

You remind me of a poem I can't remember, and a song that may never have existed, and a place I'm not sure I've ever been to.

Grampa Simpson, The Simpsons

– We met at 9.
– We met at 8.
– I was on time.
– No, you were late.
– Ah yes, I remember it well.

Maurice Chevalier and Hermione Gingold, Gigi

I'm very old – in my 90th year. I have a horrible dislike of old age. Everybody's dead – half, no nearly all of one's contemporaries – and those that aren't are gaga. Someone rang the other day and said, 'I want to invite you and Duff over for dinner.' I said, 'But Duff's been dead for 28 years.' [taps her forehead] That's what I dread.

Lady Diana Cooper

Body and mind, like man and wife, do not always agree to die together.

Peter Ouspensky

My mother is 96, and had a bad fall and a blackout a few days ago. The doctor who examined her in the A&E clearly thought she was a bit gaga, so asked her to count down from 20. 'Better than that,' she said, 'I'll do it in French,' and got down to '*douze*' before the doctor, chastened, said, 'OK, OK.'

David Horchover

They tell you that you'll lose your mind when you grow older. What they don't tell you is that you won't miss it very much.

Malcolm Cowley

I'm not worried about senility. My grandfather said, 'When you become senile, you won't know it.'

Bill Cosby

I am in the prime of senility.

Joel C. Harris

I'm not senile. I've been like this for 50 years. So even if I do become senile, people will never know.

Martin Landis, Night Court

On the Road

DRIVING

I know it's the male menopause but I fancy a 500cc Kawasaki.

Paul Nurse

They say the first thing to go when you're old is your legs or your eyesight. It isn't true. The first thing to go is parallel parking.

Kurt Vonnegut

Mr Merton is getting on in years but he's still driving. I do worry as sometimes he forgets to indicate but he always says, 'I've lived in the same road for 40 years and I think people know where I'm going by now.'

Mrs Merton

I Stop For No Particular Reason

Car Bumper Sticker for TOGS (Terry's Old Geezers)

What is the age people reach when they decide, when they back out of the driveway, they're not looking anymore? You know how they do that? They just go, 'Well, I'm old, and I'm backing out. I survived, let's see if you can.'

Jerry Seinfeld

When renewing my driver's licence at the age of 83 I was asked if I would like to be an organ donor. I said, 'Who would want them?'

Constance Dean

I would think the less time you have left in life, the faster you should drive. I think old people should be allowed to drive their age. If you're 80, do 80. If you're 100, do 100.

Jerry Seinfeld

Dearest Warden. Front tooth broken off; look like 81-year-old pirate, so at dentist 19a. Very old – very lame – no metras [sic].

Lady Diana Cooper, note to a traffic warden left on her car windscreen

The only reason I wear glasses is for little things, like driving my car – or finding it.

Woody Allen

If money was no object the present I would like is a bleeper you can press as you enter the Ascot Racecourse car park to release a slow-moving firework enabling you to locate your vehicle. I very much regret the many hours I've spent in car parks around the world searching for my car.

Clement Freud

Grandparents and Grandchildren

Mothers bear children. Grandmothers enjoy them.

Spanish proverb

My daughter pointed out the other day, 'A granny is only a double-decker mummy.'

Jilly Cooper

We are a grandmother.

Margaret Thatcher

I can't be a grandmother. I'm too young. Grandmothers are old. They bake and they sew. I was at Woodstock! I pissed in the fields!

Karen Buckman, Parenthood

Grandparents and Grandchildren

I don't like the idea of being a 'grandmother' – old and frail and the next person to go to heaven. The result of this created image was that when I go to visit my grandchildren in Liverpool nobody offers to carry my case upstairs, and when someone's car breaks down they send for me to help push it.

Carla Lane

Where have all the grannies gone? I mean the genuine, original, 22-carat articles who wore black shawls and cameo brooches, sat in rocking chairs and smelled of camphor?

Keith Waterhouse

True grannies were never seen in shops. They were never seen anywhere except at funerals. They did not visit their grandchildren: their grandchildren visited them. They would not have anything to do with electricity – true grannies were gas driven.

Keith Waterhouse

Becoming a grandmother is great fun because you can use the kid to get back at your daughter.

Roseanne

Wrinklies' Wit and Wisdom

Grandchildren don't make me feel old. It's the knowledge that I'm married to a grandmother.

Norman Collie

Grampa Simpson: Favourite Pastimes: napping, collecting beef jerky, sending complaint letters to newspapers and politicians, going to Herman's Military Antiques Store.

The Simpsons

Perfect love sometimes does not come till the first grandchild.

Welsh proverb

What feeling in all the world is so nice as that of a child's hand in yours? What tenderness it arouses, what power it conjures. You are instantly the very touchstone of wisdom and strength.

Marjorie Holmes

The reason grandparents and grandchildren get along so well is that they have a common enemy.

Sam Levenson

Never have children, only grandchildren.

Gore Vidal

Grandparents and Grandchildren

Every generation revolts against its fathers and makes friends with its grandfathers.

Lewis Mumford

It's funny that those things your kids did that got on your nerves seem so cute when your grandchildren do them.

Raymond Holland

Does Grandpa love to babysit his grandchildren? Are you kidding? By day he is too busy taking hormone shots at the doctor's or chip shots on the golf course. At night he and Grandma are too busy doing the cha-cha.

Hal Boyle

The simplest toy, one which even the youngest child can operate, is called a grandparent.

Sam Levenson

'You're old, Nanny,' said my grandson, Tom, 'but only on the outside.'

Ellen Tate

On my 60th birthday my 4-year-old grandson asked me if I was now a 'superior citizen'.

Anon

Wrinklies' Wit and Wisdom

I was looking after my 6-year-old grandson and I suggested we go into the garden to get some potatoes to cook for dinner. He was digging away when he suddenly looked at me with a very puzzled expression, and said, 'Nana, why do you bury your potatoes?'

Pat Boucher

My grandson was proud of his newly acquired reading skills and when I took him shopping he was reading every sign in sight. 'Look Nana,' he cried, 'Men Swear – they do, don't they?'

Angie Mayer

My grandchildren take me to the beach and try to make words out of the veins in my legs.

Phyllis Diller

Seeing snow for the first time, my grandson jumped for joy and cried, 'Ooh, icing!'

Alex Lacey

I was reading a book to my young grandson, Adam, about a little girl who didn't know her manners. In the story, the mother gives her little girl a plate of hamburger and chips and says, 'What's the magic word?' 'Gravy!' comes the reply. 'What *should* she have said?' I asked. Adam didn't hesitate, 'Ketchup!'

Phyl Jarski

Playing the board-game version of *Who Wants to be a Millionaire?* with my grandchildren, a Shakespearean question came up: How many ghosts does Hamlet see? a) 1 b) 2 c) 3 d) 4. My grandson thought for a moment, then said, 'Dunno. Which play is Hamlet in?' 'Not sure,' replied my granddaughter, 'I think it was *Macbeth*.' I bought them a copy of *The Complete Works of Shakespeare* for Christmas.

Phyllis Amison

After Sunday School, my granddaughter asked thoughtfully, 'Granddad, were you in the ark?' 'Of course not!' I replied. 'Then why weren't you drowned?'

James Potter

– Gran, you gave the baby whisky?
– Yes, it's okay. I didn't let him drive.

Jimmy Cox and Grandma, Rock Me Baby

Grandparents Observed

My husband and I have decided to start a family while my parents are still young enough to look after them.

Rita Rudner

My grandmother was a very tough woman. She buried three husbands. Two of them were just napping.

Rita Rudner

Grandmother, as she gets older, is not fading, but becoming more concentrated.

Paulette Alden

I was talking to my nan about Ant and Dec. She didn't know which one Dec was. I said, 'Do you know which one Ant is?' She said, 'Yes.'

Jimmy Carr

My nan has a picture of the United Kingdom tattooed over her whole body. Some people think it's weird but you can say what you like about my nan, at least you know where you are with her.

Harry Hill

'Get Off The Gas Stove Granny You're Too Old To Ride The Range'

Song title

Grandparents Observed

The word 'good' has many meanings. For example, if a man were to shoot his grandmother at a range of 500 yards, I should call him a good shot, but not necessarily a good man.

G.K. Chesterton

Elizabeth and Margaret coined for George V the epithet, 'Grandpa England'.

Anon

As a child, I went into the study of my grandfather, Winston Churchill. 'Grandpapa,' I said, 'is it true that you are the greatest man in the world?' 'Yes, now bugger off.'

Nicholas Soames

Market research is about as accurate as my grandmother's big toe was in predicting the weather.

Garrison Keillor

I was watching the Superbowl with my 92-year-old grandfather. The team scored a touchdown. They showed the instant replay. He thought they scored another one. I was gonna tell him, but I figured the game *he* was watching was better.

Steven Wright

We used to terrorize our baby-sitters when I was little – except for my grandfather because he used to read to us from his will.

Jan Ditullio

I'm very proud of my gold pocket watch. My grandfather, on his deathbed, sold me this watch.

Woody Allen

My gently lachrymose grandmother had an extraordinary capacity for reliving the events of the Bible as though they were headline news in the paper.

Peter Ustinov

My grandmother was utterly convinced I'd wind up as the Archbishop of Canterbury. And, to be honest, I've never entirely ruled it out.

Hugh Grant

Helped Grandma with the weekend shopping. She was dead fierce in the grocer's; she watched the scales like a hawk watching a field mouse. Then she pounced and accused the shop assistant of giving her underweight bacon. The shop assistant was dead scared of her and put another slice on.

Sue Townsend, The Secret Diary of Adrian Mole
Aged 13¾

Oh, Grannie, you shouldn't be carrying all those groceries! Next time, make two trips.

Nathan Lane

My grandma was a tall, rather stately woman, with iron-grey plaited headphones and 1 yellow tooth in the middle of an otherwise vacant upper set. She was in her 70s when she came to live with us and had suffered two strokes since her arrival. My brothers used to say, 'At the third stroke, she will be 70-something.'

Julie Walters, Baby Talk

Three old grannies were sitting on a park bench talking among themselves when a flasher comes by. The flasher stood right in front of them, and opened his trench coat.

The first old granny had a stroke.

Then the second old granny had a stroke.

But the third old granny had arthritis and couldn't reach that far.

Anon

– Grampa kinda smells like that trunk in the garage where the bottom's all wet.

– Nuh-uh, he smells more like a photo lab.

– Stop it, both of you! Grampa smells like a regular old man, which is more like a hallway in a hospital.

Bart, Lisa and Homer Simpson, The Simpsons

Kids, your grandfather's ears are not gross. And they're certainly not an enchanted forest.

Lois Griffin, Family Guy

I loved my grandparents' home. Everything smelled older, worn but safe; the food aroma had baked itself into the furniture.

Susan Strasberg

My Hungarian grandfather was the kind of man that could follow someone into a revolving door and come out first.

Stephen Fry

There's one thing about children: they never go around showing snapshots of their grandparents.

Bessie & Beulah

Everyone's Favourite Grandmother

QUEEN ELIZABETH, THE QUEEN MOTHER (1900–2002)

The Queen Mother seemed incapable of a bad performance as a national grandmother –

warm, smiling, human, understanding, she embodied everything the public could want of its grandmother.

John Pearson

– I'm going to live to be 100.
– Then it will be Charles who'll send you your centenarian telegram.

The Queen Mother and Queen Elizabeth II

I've got to go and see the old folk.

The Queen Mother, 97, spotting a group of pensioners at Cheltenham Racecourse

Is it me or are pensioners getting younger these days?

The Queen Mother, 100, presenting prizes at an old people's garden competition

Horse racing is one of the real sports that's left to us: a bit of danger and excitement, and the horses, which are the best thing in the world.

The Queen Mother

I keep a thermos flask full of champagne. It's one of my little treats.

The Queen Mother

There is all the difference in the world between the patient's meaning of the word 'comfortable' and the surgeon's.

The Queen Mother after she was described as
'comfortable' following an operation

Choppers have changed my life as conclusively as that of Anne Boleyn.

The Queen Mother on helicopters

When one is 18, one has very definite dislikes, but as one grows older, one becomes more tolerant, and finds that nearly everyone is, in some degree, nice.

The Queen Mother

She is a law unto herself and takes no notice of advice.

Aide to the Queen Mother

A glass of wine with lunch? Is that wise? You know you have to reign all afternoon.

The Queen Mother to Queen Elizabeth II

– Who do you think you are?
– Mummy, the Queen.

The Queen Mother and Queen Elizabeth II

Everyone's Favourite Grandmother

For goodness' sake, don't let Mummy have another drink.

Queen Elizabeth II to a pageboy

Don't retouch my wrinkles in the photograph. I would not want it to be thought that I had lived for all these years without having anything to show for it.

The Queen Mother

I love life, that's my secret.

The Queen Mother

Hers was a great old age, but not a cramped one. She remained young at heart, and the young themselves sensed that.

Dr George Carey, Archbishop of Canterbury

She seemed gloriously unstoppable and ever since I was a child I adored her. Her houses were always filled with an atmosphere of fun, laughter and affection.

Prince Charles

Anything that was meant to be formal and went wrong, she enjoyed. She laughed herself stupid about it. It kept us all sane. She loved to hear about my friends and all they got up to. And she loved to hear about how much trouble I got into at school.

Prince William

She saw the funny side of life and we laughed till we cried. Oh, how I shall miss those laughs and the wonderful wisdom born of so much experience and of an innate sensitivity to life.

Prince Charles

My favourite photograph of us together is a picture of me aged about 9 or 10 helping the Queen Mother up the steps of Windsor Castle. I remember the moment because she said to me: 'Keep doing that for people and you will go a long way in life.'

Prince William

– One Christmas, we were sitting watching Ali G on TV. We were laughing when my great-grandmother came in. She saw Ali G click his fingers and say 'Respec', and Harry and I showed her what to do. After three goes she had it. Later that day, when we were all having Christmas lunch, she tried it out.
– It was the end of the meal, and she stood up and said, 'Darling, lunch was marvellous –

respec',' and clicked her fingers. Everyone
burst out laughing.

Prince William and Prince Harry

Before I went to St Andrew's, she gave me a
farewell lunch. As she said goodbye, she said,
'Any good parties, invite me down.' But there
was no way. I knew full well that if I invited her
down, she would dance me under the table.

Prince William

She was, quite simply, the most magical
grandmother you could possibly have.

Prince Charles

Parents and Children

Avenge yourself, live long enough to be a
problem to your children.

Kirk Douglas

All right, since your parents are coming, I did
the standard preparent sweep. Which means if
you're looking for your 'neck massager' it's
under the bed.

Jimmy Cox, Rock Me Baby

– Homer, are you really going to ignore your
  father for the rest of your life?
– Of course not, Marge, just for the rest of his
  life.

Marge and Homer Simpson, The Simpsons

You might notice your ageing parents have both
become abnormally attached to some kind of
pet, a dog or a cat that they got after all the kids
left home. They buy it sweaters and birthday
gifts and they have conversations with it that are
often longer and more meaningful than the
ones they have with you.

Dave Barry

– Dorothy, why don't we bond?
– Mom, we're from before bonding and quality
  time.

Dorothy Zbornak and Sophia Petrillo, The Golden Girls

Stay another bloody week? Over my dead body!
She makes me un-bloody-plug everything at
night before we go to bed – but she's got herself
a bloody electric blanket on all night.

Jim Royle, The Royle Family

– You must miss Prince Andrew, Ma'am, when
  he's away in the Navy?

– Indeed I do. Especially because he is the only one in the family who knows how to work the video.

Visitor and Queen Elizabeth II

My parents did a really scary thing recently. They bought a caravan. This means that they can pull up in front of my house anytime now and just live there.

Paula Poundstone

My parents live in a retirement community, which is basically a minimum-security prison with a golf course.

Joel Warshaw

Why do so many old people live in those minimum-security prisons? What's with all the security? Are the old people trying to escape, or are people stealing old people?

Jerry Seinfeld

Knowing as I do Frasier's relationship with his father, when he informed me he had taken him in to live with him, I immediately flipped to the weather channel to see if hell had indeed frozen over.

Lilith Sternen, Frasier

– It seems like only yesterday that Dad moved in with you.
– Isn't it interesting that two people can have completely opposite impressions of the same event.

Niles and Frasier Crane, Frasier

– Onslow, Father's on the roof again!
– Ask him if he's got my bottle opener!

Rose and Onslow, Keeping Up Appearances

From the vantage point of his wondrously serene old age, my father contemplates our lives almost as if they were books he can dip into whenever he wants. His back pages, perhaps.

Angela Carter

As you get older, your dad gets smaller. When I went home last time, he'd practically disappeared.

Jeff Green

My father has lived so long that everything is forgiven, even his habit of referring to the present incumbent by my first husband's name.

Angela Carter

Parents and Children

No matter how old a mother is, she watches her middle-aged children for signs of improvement.

Florida Scott-Maxwell

I am 102 years of age. I have no worries since my youngest son went into an old folk's home.

Victoria Bedwell

Children are a great comfort in your old age. They help you reach it faster, too.

Lionel Kauffman

My parents just arrived back from Singapore on the *QE2* and invited me for dinner on board the ship. 'So,' my father said, leaning back in the antique chair with a smug expression, 'enjoying your inheritance? I know I am.' He and my mother couldn't stop laughing.

Chris McEvoy

Your kids will forgive you someday. Of course, by then you'll be dead.

Sophia Petrillo, The Golden Girls

Always be nice to your children, because they are the ones who will choose your rest home.

Phyllis Diller

Twilight Homes for the Bewildered

Retirement homes are great. It's like being a baby, only you're old enough to appreciate it.

Homer Simpson, The Simpsons

The colour brochure for the Dunraven Sunset Facility showed artists' impressions of cleanly dressed oldsters watching TV and Zimmering around in rose gardens, smiling like those people you see on the Air Safety card as they slither down emergency chutes or calmly inflate each other's whistles.

Dame Edna Everage

I've got a placement as a volunteer at an old folk's day centre. They've got this 'companion scheme' where we chat informatively to the old-timers about the issues of the day, and in return they sort of tell us stories about rationing and how chicken used to taste like chicken.

Tony, Men Behaving Badly

Nursing homes. Ugh. I hate those places. All the old people want to touch my hair.

Claire Fisher, Six Feet Under

I could smell the funny odour rest homes always seem to have: a mixture of roast lamb, chloroform and little jobs.

Dame Edna Everage

My mother's suffering from advanced old-timer's disease so we've put her in a maximum-security Twilight Home for the Bewildered. Her accommodation is in the Sylvia Plath Suite. Other wards include the Virginia Woolf Incontinence Wing, the Diane Arbus X-ray Unit, and the Zelda Fitzgerald Fire Escape.

Dame Edna Everage

My First 100 Years

On 14 January, Rose will be 100 years old, and she's looking forward to receiving a telegram from the Queen. It seems a scant reward for what is, after all, a century. Come on Queen Elizabeth, give us some incentive!

Mrs Merton

I don't want to live to be a 100. I don't think I could stand to see bell bottom trousers three times.

Jeff Foxworthy

Wrinklies' Wit and Wisdom

Who wants to live to be 100? Anyone who's 99.

Billy Wilder

If you live to be 100, I want to live to be 100 minus one day, so I never have to live without you.

Winnie the Pooh

Turning 100 was the worst birthday of my life. I wouldn't wish it on my worst enemy. Turning 101 was not so bad. Once you're past that century mark, it's just not shocking.

Bessie Delany

If I'd known I was gonna live this long, I'd have taken better care of myself.

Eubie Blake, 100

Research shows that centenarians are the healthiest group of people in the world. How do you think they got to be 100 years old? Because they don't get sick.

John Stark

Yes I'm 100. I put it down to 30 years of safe sex and boneless fish.

Annie Miller

You can live to be 100 by giving up all the things that make you want to live to be 100.

Woody Allen

A centenarian is a person who has lived to be 100 years of age. He never smoked or he smoked all his life. He never drank whiskey or he drank whiskey for 80 years. He was a vegetarian or he wasn't a vegetarian. Follow these rules closely and you too can become a centenarian.

Stephen Leacock

One thing that unites all centenarians is that they have wonderful senses of humour. They use it for all kinds of things, like joking about death. The thought of dying is no big deal. They've had time to prepare.

Margery Silver

I have been asked to pose for *Penthouse* on my 100th birthday. Everybody is going to be sorry.

Dolly Parton

Secrets of Long Life

– To what do you attribute your long life?
– To the fact that I haven't died yet.

Sir Malcolm Sargent

To what do I attribute my longevity? Bad luck mostly.

Billy Wilder

My father died at 102. Whenever I would ask what kept him going, he'd answer, 'I never worry.'

Jerry Stiller

– Happy 103rd Birthday, Mr Zukor. What is the secret of your long life?
– I gave up smoking two years ago.

Adolph Zukor

Good Things About Being the Oldest Person in the World: You make *The Guinness Book of Records* without doing a damn thing; at your 100th-year high school reunion, you've got the buffet all to yourself; you don't need denture cleaner – you can just call the grandchildren and borrow theirs; you can suck at golf and still shoot your age; you can smoke all you damn well please.

David Letterman

Bad Things About Being the Oldest Person in the World: seems like every time you turn around that damn Halley's Comet is back; shoulder-length ear hair; you get to see your great-great-great-grandchildren marry moon men; all the shoes.

David Letterman

It's a proven fact: gardeners live longer. You are young at any age if you are planning for tomorrow and gardeners are always looking forward, anticipating new shoots.

Mira Nair

You live longer once you realize that any time spent being unhappy is wasted.

Ruth E. Renkl

Women don't live longer. It just seems longer.

Erma Bombeck

Scientists say that women who have children after 40 are more likely to live to be 100, but they don't know why. I think the reason is, they're waiting for the day when their kids move out the house.

Lorrie Moss

— What is your prescription for a healthy long life?
— Never deny yourself anything.

Mr Justice Holmes

Ciggie-loving Marie Ellis was laid to rest yesterday — after living to 105 despite smoking nearly half a million fags. She was cremated clutching a packet of her favourite Benson &

Hedges. Staff and residents from the nursing home sent her off with a chorus of 'Smoke Gets In Your Eyes'.

Sun newspaper

Alcohol is good for you. My grandfather proved it irrevocably. He drank two quarts of booze every mature day of his life and lived to the age of 103. I was at the cremation – the fire would not go out.

Dave Astor

I can only assume that it is largely due to the accumulation of toasts to my health over the years that I am still enjoying a fairly satisfactory state of health and have reached such an unexpectedly great age.

The Duke of Edinburgh, 80

My three rules for a long life are regular exercise, hobbies and complete avoidance of midget gems.

Kitty, Victoria Wood

I credit my youthfulness at 80 to the fact of a cheerful disposition and contentment in every period of my life with what I was.

Oliver Wendell Holmes

At 70, I'm in fine fettle for my age, sleep like a babe and feel around 12. The secret? Lots of meat, drink and cigarettes and not giving in to things.

Jennifer Paterson

The secret of my long life? Swim, dance a little, go to Paris every August, and live within walking distance of two hospitals.

Dr Horatio Luro

My grandmother just passed away, she was 104 years old. I went to buy some flowers and the guy there says, 'Ooh, 104? How'd she die?' *How'd she die?* She was 104! I told him, 'Well, it's alright – they saved the baby.'

Larry the Cable Guy

I attribute my long and healthy life to the fact that I never touched a cigarette, a drink, or a girl until I was 10 years old.

George Moore

– What is the secret of your long life?
– Keep breathing.

Sophie Tucker

Wrinklies' Wit and Wisdom

If you want a long life, several years before birth, advertise for a couple of parents belonging to long-lived families.

Oliver Wendell Holmes

No one's so old that he doesn't think he could hope for one more day.

Seneca

If you survive long enough, you're revered – rather like an old building.

Katharine Hepburn

If you live to be 90 in England and can still eat a boiled egg, they think you deserve the Nobel Prize.

Alan Bennett

A Grand Old Man is anyone with snow-white hair who has kept out of jail till 80.

Stephen Leacock

I've never known a person who lives to 110 who is remarkable for anything else.

Josh Billings

Great men, men who change the world don't usually die of old age. Somebody kills them. Think of Jesus, Martin Luther King Jr, JFK.

D.H. Hughley

– You've reached the ripe old age of 121. What do you expect the future will be like?
– Very short.

Interviewer and Jeanne Calment (1875–1997)

The Oldest Swinger in Town

LOVE AND COURTSHIP

Your place, or back to the sheltered accommodation?

Barry Cryer

Hi, I'm Marv, your grandmother's gentleman-caller, or as you kids would say, her booty call.

Marv, Rock Me Baby

'When My Love Comes Back From The Ladies' Room Will I Be Too Old To Care?'

Lewis Grizzard, song title

They say a man is as old as the woman he feels. In that case, I'm 85.

Groucho Marx

Only flirt with women who flirt with you or you can end up looking like those old rich gents in night-clubs, proudly photographed

with their arms round bimbos whose interest
was clearly in the old geezer's bank balance
rather than in his wrinkled and lined person.

George Melly

Hugh Hefner now has 7 girlfriends – one for
each day of the week. Someone needs to tell
him that those are nurses.

Jay Leno

When we were young, you made me blush,
go hot and cold, and turn to mush.
I still feel all these things, it's true –
but is it menopause, or you?

Susan Anderson

As you get older, the pickings get slimmer, but
the people don't.

Carrie Fisher

Gentleman, retired, knocking on a bit. Own
teeth and hair. Seeks lady (45 plus) for raw sex.

Lonely hearts ad

Before I turn 67, I would like to have a lot of
sex with a man I like. If you want to talk first,
Trollope works for me.

Jane Juska, personal ad, New York Times
Review of Books

The Oldest Swinger in Town

I was introduced to a beautiful young lady as a gentleman in his 90s. *Early* 90s, I insisted.

George Burns

Delighted you came, my dear, and I'd like you to know that you made a happy man feel very old.

Terry-Thomas, The Last Remake of Beau Geste

— You wrote in a story that when you reached the age of 84 you would commit suicide. Why have you not done so?
— Laziness and cowardice prevent me. Besides, I am constantly falling in love.

Jorge Luis Borges

It's never too late to have a fling
For Autumn is just as nice as Spring
And it's never too late to fall in love.

Sandy Wilson

Nothing makes people crosser than being considered too old for love.

Nancy Mitford

I have almost done with harridans, and shall soon become old enough to fall in love with girls of 14.

Jonathan Swift

Wrinklies' Wit and Wisdom

When one is 20, yes, but at 47, Venus may rise from the sea, and I for one should hardly put on my spectacles to have a look.

William Thackeray

Trouble is, by the time you can read a girl like a book, your library card has expired.

Milton Berle

Age does not protect you from love. But love, to some extent, protects you from age.

Jeanne Moreau

Those who love deeply never grow old; they may die of old age, but they die young.

Benjamin Franklin

The lovely thing about being 40 is that you can appreciate 25-year-old men more.

Colleen McCullough

There ain't nothin' an ol' man can do but bring me a message from a young one.

'Moms' Mabley

I think older women with younger men threaten all the right people.

William Hamilton

The Oldest Swinger in Town

The advantages of dating younger men is that on them everything, like hair and teeth, is in the right place as opposed to being on the bedside table or bathroom floor.

Candace Bushnell

I don't date women my own age. There aren't any.

Milton Berle

The older woman's love is not love of herself, nor of herself mirrored in a lover's eyes, nor is it corrupted by need. It is a feeling of tenderness so still and deep and warm that it gilds every grass blade and blesses every fly. I wouldn't have missed it for the world.

Germaine Greer

I thought nobody would touch me again – not until the undertaker.

May, The Mother

– I do love the rain so. It reminds me of my first kiss.
– Ah, your first kiss was in the rain?
– No, it was in the shower.

Blanche Devereaux and Dorothy Zbornak,
The Golden Girls

Learning to love yourself is the greatest love of all, says George Benson in the popular song. I learned to love myself in the early 1980s and have never looked back.

Mrs Merton

Marriage

When marrying, ask yourself this question: do you believe that you will be able to converse well with this person into your old age? Everything else in marriage is transitory.

Friedrich Nietzsche

It's quite a romantic idea, growing old together. Sitting on park benches, feeding the ducks, leafing gently through *Saga* magazine.

Dorothy, Men Behaving Badly

Walking down the aisle together after they'd just married, Michael Denison turned to his new wife Dulcie Gray and whispered, 'Just think, darling, only 50 years off our golden wedding anniversary!' He died just before they reached their 60th anniversary.

Alan Marks

Marriage

I want to be married to my wife until we forget
each other's names. My wife is the only one
who knows what I used to be; and she is starting
to lose a little of it too, so we are breaking down
in tandem.

Bill Cosby

An archaeologist is the best husband a woman
can have; the older she gets, the more interested
he is in her.

Agatha Christie

Whatever you may look like, marry a man your
own age – as your beauty fades, so will his
eyesight.

Phyllis Diller

Carol Channing, 82, star of the hit musical, *Hello,
Dolly!*, wrote fondly about her high school
sweetheart, Harry Kullijian, in her memoir, *Just
Lucky*. Kullijian, 83, read the book, got in touch
with Carol, and now they've got married. 'He's
exactly the same now as he was when we were
12,' said Ms Channing.

Amy Robinson

We've managed 24 years of marriage – with a
lot of broken crockery along the way.

Eileen Atkins

Wrinklies' Wit and Wisdom

My wife and I have just celebrated our 30th wedding anniversary. If I had killed her the first time I thought about it, I'd be out of prison by now.

Frank Carson

My parents have a very good marriage. They've been together forever. They've passed their silver and gold anniversaries. The next one is rust.

Rita Rudner

I gave him the best years of my thighs.

Dorothy Zbornak, The Golden Girls

My parents stayed together for 40 years but that was out of spite.

Woody Allen

I've been married so long I'm on my third bottle of Tabasco.

Susan Vass

The best way to get a husband to do anything is to suggest that he is too old to do it.

Felicity Parker

When you live with another person for 50 years, all your memories are invested in that person, like a bank account of shared memories. Thus, the past is part of the present as long as the other person lives. It is better than any scrapbook, because you are both living scrapbooks.

Federico Fellini

Love is what you've been through with somebody.

James Thurber

My notion of a wife at 40 is that a man should be able to change her, like a bank note, for two 20s.

Douglas Jerrold

I wouldn't be caught dead marrying a woman old enough to be my wife.

Tony Curtis

When a man of 60 runs off with a young woman, I'm never surprised. I have a sneaking admiration for him. After all, he's going to need it.

Deborah Kerr

He has a future and I have a past, so we should be all right.

Jennie Churchill, 64, marrying Montagu Porch, 41

When people ask me, *sotto voce* in surprise, 'So what about the age difference between you and your husband, Percy?' I usually shrug, smile and quip, 'So, if he dies, he dies.'

Joan Collins

You're too old to get married again. Not only can't you cut the mustard, honey, you're too old to open the jar.

Bob Hope

I was once engaged when I was 40, and I found it gave me very serious constipation. So I broke off the engagement and the lady quite understood.

Fellow of Trinity College, Cambridge, 97

Being an old maid is like death by drowning – a really delightful sensation after you have ceased struggling.

Edna Ferber

Sex

A little old lady in the nursing home holds up her clenched fist and announces, 'Anyone who can guess what I have in my closed hand can have sex with me tonight.' An elderly gentleman calls out, 'An elephant.' 'Close enough,' she replies.

Anon

When the grandmothers of today hear the word 'Chippendales', they don't necessarily think of chairs.

Jean Kerr

I haven't yet reached the stage where I'd agree that liniment oil is a decent replacement for sex.

Stephanie Beacham

It's ill-becoming for an old broad to sing about how bad she wants it. But occasionally we do.

Lena Horne

– There's a man on our lawn.
– Get a net!

Dorothy Zbornak and Blanche Devereaux, The Golden Girls

Let's do it! Let's do it! I really want to rant
   and rave.
Let's go, 'cause I know, just how I want you to
   behave:
Not bleakly. Not meekly.

Wrinklies' Wit and Wisdom

Beat me on the bottom with a *Woman's
Weekly*.
Let's do it! Let's do it! Let's do it tonight!

Victoria Wood

Pass me my teeth, and I'll bite you.

George Burns

An old broom knows the dirty corners best.

Irish proverb

My mother-in-law was on holiday in Italy with
friends in a villa situated at the end of an unlit,
perilous path. A torch was found to light the
way but it had no batteries. 'I know,' said my
mother-in-law's friend, a lady in her early 60s,
'I'll use the ones out of my vibrator.'

Janice Turner

Of all the faculties, the last to leave us is sexual
desire. That means that long after wearing
bifocals and hearing aids, we'll still be making
love. We just won't know with whom.

Jack Paar

If you cannot catch a bird of paradise, better
take a wet hen.

Russian proverb

The great thing about sex when you're older is that you don't have to worry about getting pregnant.

Barbra Streisand

I can still enjoy sex at 75. I live at 76, so it's no distance.

Bob Monkhouse

There's a lot of promiscuity about these days, and I'm all for it.

Ben Travers, 94

In the theatre I'm playing, there's a hole in the wall between the ladies' dressing room and mine. I've been meaning to plug it up, but what the hell ... let 'em enjoy themselves.

George Burns, 82

On my 85th birthday, I felt like a 20-year-old. But there wasn't one around.

Milton Berle

I prefer young girls. Their stories are shorter.

Thomas McGuane

At my age I like threesomes – in case one of us dies.

Rodney Dangerfield

Wrinklies' Wit and Wisdom

I think that Viagra and the Pill are the two most important inventions of the second half of the 20th century.

Hugh Hefner

Now that I'm 78, I do tantric sex because it's very slow. My favourite position is called the plumber. You stay in all day but nobody comes.

John Mortimer

I'm 78 but I still use a condom when I have sex. I can't take the damp.

Alan Gregory

Just because you're in your 70s doesn't mean you can't still swing. All the old geezers throw their false teeth onto the table, the ladies pick a set and hook up with the owner.

Anon

People are startled by my books because they think, how can an old woman write about sex? The idea that people go on being sexy all their life is little explored in fiction. What do people think 'happy ever after' means? It goes on and on; it doesn't end.

Mary Wesley

As I grow older and older and totter towards the tomb, I find that I care less and less who goes to bed with whom.

Dorothy L. Sayers

I'm at the stage of life when I'd give up a night of wild rapture with Denzel Washington for a nice report on my next bone density test.

Judith Viorst

In my mid-60s, what I find the hardest to bear is being 'safe'. After a gym session I found myself in the Jacuzzi with a gorgeous young brunette. We had a wonderful chat, laughing and joking. But it was awful. Sitting there in her skimpy bikini, she did not see me as even slightly dangerous.

Peter Church

I have no sex appeal. A Peeping Tom saw me and pulled down the shade.

Phyllis Diller

I'm getting old. When I squeeze into a tight parking space, I'm sexually satisfied for the day.

Rodney Dangerfield

Sex and death. Two things that come once in a lifetime. But at least after death you are not nauseous.

Woody Allen

Use it or lose it.

Joan Collins

I haven't had sex since 1959. Of course it's only 21:00 now.

Tom O'Connor

My sex life is now reduced to fan letters from an elderly lesbian who wants to borrow 800 dollars.

Groucho Marx

If it weren't for speed bumps, pickpockets and frisking at airports, I'd have no sex life at all.

Rodney Dangerfield

Nowadays I reserve my sexual activities for special occasions such as the installation of a new Pope.

Dave Barry

If it wasn't for the rectal probe I'd have no sex life at all.

Barry Cryer

After 50, litigation takes the place of sex.

Gore Vidal

– Your fly-buttons are undone.
– No matter. The dead bird does not fall out of
  the nest.

Winston Churchill

As a young man, I used to have four supple
members and one stiff one. Now I have four
stiff and one supple.

Henri Duc D'Aumale

I'm going to Iowa to collect an award. Then
I'm appearing at Carnegie Hall, it's sold out.
Then I'm sailing to France to pick up an
honour from the French government. I'd give it
all up for one erection.

Groucho Marx

God gives nuts to those who have no teeth.

Arabic proverb

To succeed with the opposite sex, tell her you're
impotent. She can't wait to disprove it.

Cary Grant, 72

If the devil were to offer me a resurgence of
what is commonly called virility, I'd decline. 'Just
keep my liver and lungs in good working order,'
I'd reply, 'so I can go on drinking and smoking.'

Luis Buñuel

A medical report states that the human male is physically capable of enjoying sex up to and even beyond the age of 80. Not as a participant of course …

Denis Norden

Sex after 90 is like trying to shoot pool with a rope. I'm at that age now where just putting my cigar in its holder is a thrill.

George Burns

Like being unchained from a lunatic.

Sophocles on his declining sexual powers

Lord, give me chastity – but not yet.

St Augustine

Work

In the days when I went to work, I never once knew what I was doing. These days, I never work. Work does age one so.

Quentin Crisp

Age to me means nothing. I can't get old while I'm working. I was old when I was 21 and out of work. As long as you're working, you stay young.

George Burns

If you keep working you'll last longer and I just want to keep vertical. I'd hate to spend the rest of my life trying to outwit an 18-inch fish.

Harold S. Geneen

I'm too old for a paper round, too young for social security and too tired for an affair.

Erma Bombeck

I am delighted to find that even at my age great ideas come to me, the pursuit and development of which should require another lifetime.

Johann Wolfgang von Goethe

Very few people do anything creative after the age of 35. The reason is that very few people do anything creative before the age of 35.

Joel Hildebrand

Like the old pro said, it's not the work, it's the stairs.

Elaine Stritch

How can I die? I'm booked!

George Burns

The Gold Watch

RETIREMENT

I'm taking early retirement. I want my share of Social Security before the whole system goes bust.

David Letterman

I have made enough noise in the world already, perhaps too much, and am now getting old, and want retirement.

Napoleon Bonaparte

It is time I stepped aside for a less experienced and less able man.

Scott Elledge

When a man falls into his anecdotage, it is a sign for him to retire from the world.

Benjamin Disraeli

I really think that it's better to retire, in Uncle Earl's terms, when you still have some snap left in your garters.

Russell B. Long

The Gold watch

I know how we'll end up in our dotage – my cat, Vienna, stretched across a tennis racket, and me in the local library clinging to the radiators.

Rigsby, Rising Damp

Abolish the retirement age. After all, if everyone had to stop working when they reached 65, Winston Churchill would not have been our wartime leader. He was 66 when he became Prime Minister.

Daily Mirror

We spend our lives on the run. We get up by the clock, eat and sleep by the clock, get up again, go to work, and then we retire. And what do they give us? A bloody clock.

Dave Allen

Sometimes it's better to be sacked. I hate the leaving do, and the statutory retirement present, which is always something awful like a gold watch or an engraved wok.

Greg Dyke

Musicians don't retire; they stop when there's no more music in them.

Louis Armstrong

Wrinklies' Wit and Wisdom

I'll never retire. I won't quit the business until I get run over by a truck, a producer or a critic.

Jack Lemmon

Retire? Did Christ come down from the Cross?

Pope John Paul II

There comes a time when it is too late to retire.

Lord Hailsham

I'm retired. I'm now officially a lower form of life than a Duracell battery. I've been replaced by a box. It's standard procedure apparently for a man my age. The next stage is to stick you inside one.

Victor Meldrew, One Foot in the Grave

After I retired, I fished a lot, dove a lot, boated a lot – and made Johnny Walker Red about a quarter of a million dollars richer.

Dennis Diaz

What do gardeners do when they retire?

Bob Monkhouse

What shall I do now I'm retired? I thought I might grow a beard … give me something to do.

Victor Meldrew, One Foot in the Grave

The Gold watch

I make the coffee, Barbara makes the beds, and we're right back to square one where we got married when we were 20 years old.

George Bush, former US President

My husband has just retired. I married him for better or for worse, but not for lunch.

Hazel Weiss

A retired husband is often a wife's full-time job.

Ella Harris

If I had to retire I'd probably bore my wife to tears. The commonest sight, now that people retire earlier and live much longer, is of couples walking round supermarkets, the wives filling the trolleys, the men carrying lists and saying: 'Why are you buying this?'

Terry Wogan

It's very hard to make a home for a man if he's always in it.

Winifred Kirkland

The important thing about women today is, as they get older, they still keep house. It's one reason why they don't die, but men die when they retire. Women just polish the teacups.

Margaret Mead

I don't even think about a retirement programme because I'm working for the Lord, for the Almighty. And even though the Lord's pay isn't very high, his retirement programme is, you might say, out of this world.

George Foreman

Time Flies

One day, aged 45, I just went into the kitchen to make myself a cup of tea, and when I came out I found I was 68.

Thora Hird

One day a bachelor, the next a grampa. What is the secret of the trick? How did I get so old so quick?

Ogden Nash

As I get older the years just fly by. I don't think there was an April this year.

Jeremy Hardy

Years grow shorter but days grow longer. When you're over 70, a day is an awful lot of time.

Carl Sandburg

Guinness is a great day-shortener. If you get out
of bed first thing and drink a glass then the day
doesn't begin until about 12.30, when you
come to again, which is nice. I try to live in a
perpetual snooze.

Quentin Crisp

Men talk of killing time, while time quietly kills
them.

Dion Boucicault

Half our life is spent trying to find something to
do with the time we have rushed through life
trying to save.

Will Rogers

No matter how much time you save, at the end of
your life, there's no extra time saved up. You'll be
going, 'What do you mean there's no time? I had
a microwave oven, Velcro sneakers, a clip-on tie.
Where's the time?' But there isn't any. Because
when you waste time in life, they subtract it. Like
if you saw *all* the Rocky movies, they deduct that.

Jerry Seinfeld

There is never enough time, unless you're
serving it.

Malcolm Forbes

Whenever I get down about life going by too quickly, what helps me is a little mantra that I repeat to myself: at least I'm not a fruit fly.

Ray Romano

Don't be over-impressed by time. Accept it, but don't kowtow to it. We should still be able to stick two fingers in the air as the diminishing amount of sand trickles through the hourglass.

George Melly

Carpe Diem

When one subtracts from life infancy (which is vegetation), sleep, eating and swilling, buttoning and unbuttoning – how much remains of downright existence? The summer of a dormouse.

Lord Byron

For every person who has ever lived there has come, at last, a spring he will never see. Glory then in the springs that are yours.

Pam Brown

Life will be over sooner than we think. If we have bikes to ride and people to love, now is the time.

Elisabeth Kübler-Ross

If you were going to die soon and had only one phone call you could make, who would you call and what would you say? And why are you waiting?

Stephen Levine

Most of us spend our lives as if we had another one in the bank.

Ben Irwin

One of the most tragic things I know about human nature is that all of us tend to put off living. We are all dreaming of some magical rose garden over the horizon – instead of enjoying the roses that are blooming outside our windows today.

Dale Carnegie

Even a great feast has a last course.

Chinese proverb

At 87, 'someday' and 'one of these days' are losing their grip on my vocabulary; if it's worth seeing or hearing or doing, I want to see and hear and do it now.

Anon

Don't ever save anything for a special occasion. Being alive is the special occasion.

Avril Sloe

Wrinklies' Wit and Wisdom

Don't save things 'for best'. Drink that vintage bottle of wine – from your best crystal glasses. Wear your best designer jacket to go down to the post office to collect your pension. And, every morning, spritz yourself with that perfume you save for parties.

Geraldine Mayer

I've decided life is too fragile to finish a book I dislike just because it cost $16.95 and everyone else loved it. Or eat a fried egg with a broken yolk (which I hate) when the dog would leap over the St Louis Arch for it.

Erma Bombeck

Life is too short to learn German.

Richard Porson

Dust if you must, but wouldn't it be better,
To paint a picture or write a letter,
Bake a cake or plant a seed,
Ponder the difference between want and
   need?

Dust if you must, but there's not much time,
With rivers to swim and mountains to climb,
Music to hear and books to read,
Friends to cherish and life to lead.

Dust if you must, but the world's out there,
With the sun in your eyes, the wind in your
    hair,
A flutter of snow, a shower of rain.
This day will not come 'round again.

Dust if you must, but bear in mind,
Old age will come and it's not always kind.
And when you go and go you must,
You, yourself, will make more dust.

Anon

Don't spend your life trying to please those who
won't cry at your funeral.

Gerald Brooks

Don't wait for pie in the sky when you die. Get
yours now, with ice cream on top!

The Reverend Ike

Enjoy yourself; it's later than you think.

Horace

Gotta Lotta Livin' To Do

There will come a time when you believe
everything is finished. That will be the beginning.

Louis L'Amour

Wrinklies' Wit and Wisdom

I want to tell people approaching and perhaps fearing age that it is a time of discovery. If they say, 'Of what?' I can only answer, 'We must find out for ourselves, otherwise it won't be a discovery.'

Florida Scott-Maxwell

Look, I don't want to wax philosophic, but I will say that if you're alive you've got to flap your arms and legs, you've got to jump around a lot, for life is the very opposite of death, and therefore you must at very least think noisy and colourfully, or you're not alive.

Mel Brooks

Let's not go out and get denture cream. Let's go to the nude beach and let our wrinkled selves hang out! We'll sit on the boardwalk and watch the old men rearrange themselves when they come out of the water.

Sophia Petrillo, The Golden Girls

Do not grow old, no matter how long you live. Never cease to stand like curious children before the Great Mystery into which we were born.

Albert Einstein

Gotta Lotta Livin' To Do

I am more alive than most people. I am an
electric eel in a pond of goldfish.

Edith Sitwell

When you're young, you don't know, but you
don't know you don't know, so you take some
chances. In your 20s and 30s you don't know,
and you know you don't know, and that tends
to freeze you; less risk taking. In your 40s you
know, but you don't know you know, so you
may still be a little tentative. But then, as you
pass 50, if you've been paying attention, you
know, and you know you know. Time for
some fun.

George Carlin

Life is a great big canvas, and you should throw
all the paint on it you can.

Danny Kaye

Write, paint, sculpt, learn the piano, take up
dancing, whether it's the tango or line-dancing,
start a college course, fall in love all over again –
the possibilities are limitless for you to achieve
your private ambitions.

Joan Collins

Singing, fishing, meeting my close and dear friends, looking at pictures and nature, shocking a few people who deserve shocking, taking my pills, writing a book and swigging Irish whiskey. These are my ways of fending off the old gent with the scythe waiting patiently to harvest me.

George Melly

I use my increased leisure time to look at paintings wherever there is a gallery, to enjoy opera and drama at a theatre, to visit country houses.

Denis Healey

Life isn't measured by how many breaths we take, but by the moments that take our breath away.

Chinese saying

Sometimes I would rather have someone take away years of my life than take away a moment.

Pearl Bailey

We should do something that will make your heart dance once a day. If you can't do that because you're too depressed, then do something that will make somebody else's heart dance.

Yoko Ono

There were days last winter when I danced for sheer joy out in my frost-bound garden in spite of my years and children. But I did it behind a bush, having a due regard for the decencies.

Elizabeth von Arnim

I get up before anyone else in my household, not because sleep has deserted me in my advancing years, but because an intense eagerness to live draws me from my bed.

Maurice Goudeket

Most people say that as you get old, you have to give up things. I think you get old because you give up things.

Theodore Green

Develop interest in life as you see it: in people, things, literature, music – the world is so rich, simply throbbing with treasures, beautiful souls and interesting people. Forget yourself.

Henry Miller

I wouldn't mind turning into vermilion goldfish.

Henri Matisse, 80

Wrinklies' Wit and Wisdom

Enjoying sex, loving fashion, having fun, decorating our homes, going on lavish holidays – the list is endless. Onward!

Joan Collins

It is a mistake to regard age as a downhill grade towards dissolution. The reverse is true. As one grows older, one climbs with surprising strides.

George Sand

You have to take time out to be old. I'm still full of piss and vinegar.

Paul Newman

If old people were to mobilize en masse they would constitute a formidable fighting force, as anyone who has ever had the temerity to try to board a bus ahead of a little old lady with an umbrella well knows.

Vera Forrester

I work every day and I want to die shouting *mierda*.

Joan Miró

I can't actually see myself putting make-up on my face at the age of 60. But I can see myself going on a camel train to Samarkand.

Glenda Jackson, actress

At past 50, I solemnly and painfully learned to ride the bicycle.

Henry Adams

You should make a point of trying every experience once, excepting incest and folk-dancing.

Anon

I hope I have a young outlook. Since I have an old everything else, this is my one chance of having a bit of youth as a part of me.

Richard Armour

In a boat I lost 20 or 30 years straight away.

Helen Tew, 89, trans-Atlantic sailor

The only time I've ever been rendered speechless with fury was when some daft television presenter opened a programme aimed at senior travellers by asking what sort of holidays were 'suitable' for them. 'Any and all they really want to take,' is the short answer.

Elisabeth de Stroumillo

Cruising: if you thought you didn't like people on land …

Carol Leifer

Wrinklies' Wit and Wisdom

Signs You're on a Bad Cruise: the brochure boasts the ship was the subject of a *60 Minutes* exposé; as you board, a personal injury lawyer hands you his business card; no matter what you order from the bar, it tastes of salt; every time you see the crew, they're wearing life-jackets; the vessel's name is the S.S. *Scurvy*.

David Letterman

I'd like to learn to ski but I'm 44 and I'm worried about my knees. They creak a lot and I'm afraid they might start an avalanche.

Jonathan Ross

I now realize that the small hills you see on ski-slopes are formed around the bodies of 47-year-olds who tried to learn snowboarding.

Dave Barry

There isn't anybody who doesn't like to see an old man make a comeback. Jimmy Connors seemed like a jerk to me until he was 40. After that, I rooted for him all the time. How could you not?

T. Boone Pickens

Golfers grow old and try to shoot their age. It must be a terrific feeling when someone asks your age and you can say, 'Par.'

The Pittsburgh Post

The older you get, the stronger the wind gets —
and it's always in your face.

Jack Nicklaus

You're never too old. A person of 60 can grow
as much as a child of 6. Michelangelo did some
of his best paintings when past 80; George
Bernard Shaw was still writing plays at 90;
Grandma Moses didn't even begin painting
until she was 79.

Maxwell Naltz

I don't want to get to the end of my life and
find that I lived just the length of it. I want to
have lived the width of it as well.

Diane Ackerman

Life is either a daring adventure, or nothing.

Helen Keller

Dance as if no one were watching, sing as if no
one were listening, and live every day as if it
were your last.

Tish Provest

Do not go gently into that good night,
Old age should burn and rage at close of day …

Dylan Thomas

There is sleeping enough in the grave.

Irish saying

A Quiet Life

I once wanted to save the world. Now I just want to leave the room with some dignity.

Lotus Weinstock

As I grow old, I find myself less and less inclined to take the stairs two at a time.

Bernard Baruch

I turn 70 this year and all of a sudden the horizon that once seemed far away looms right there in front of you. You feel an irresistible urge to slow down, to take your foot off the accelerator, touch it to the brake – gently, but surely – and start negotiating yourself out of the fast lane.

Bill Moyers, former White House Press Secretary

I am 72 years of age, at which period there come over one a shameful love of ease and repose, common to dogs, horses, clergymen and even to *Edinburgh Reviewers*. Then an idea comes across me that I am entitled to 5 or 6 years of quiet before I die.

Rev. Sydney Smith

Even under a harsh God, one is entitled to serenity in old age.

Albert Outler

What is wrong with settling down with a good book into a rocking chair by the fireside, wearing a comfy pair of slippers if that is what makes you happy?

Eloise Pagett

I love this time of day. When I'm sitting here in my own little home, with my own wonderful little hubby, and we talk about issues of the day and discuss world affairs and generally just snuggle.

Mavis Wilton, Coronation Street

I used to have a sign over my computer that read, 'Old Dogs Can Learn New Tricks', but lately I sometimes ask myself how many more tricks I *want* to learn. Wouldn't it be easier to be outdated?

Ram Dass

Wrinklies' Wit and Wisdom

If old age in the shape of waning strength says to me often, 'Thou shalt not!', so do my years smile upon me and say to me, 'Thou needst not!'

Mary Vorse

It's only natural that a person becomes quieter as they grow older. They've got more to keep quiet about.

Samuel Butler

One's first step to wisdom is to question everything – and one's last is to come to terms with everything.

Georg Christoph Lichtenberg

Growing older, I have lost the need to be political, which means, in this country, the need to be left. I am driven into grudging toleration of the Conservative Party because it is the party of non-politics, of resistance to politics.

Kingsley Amis

When one has reached 81, one likes to sit back and let the world turn by itself, without trying to push it.

Sean O'Casey

The members seated in the Pavilion at the Test Match declined to join in the Mexican Wave.

Well, when you get to a certain age, every time you just get out of your chair, it's a bit of an adventure.

Henry Blofeld

Old men are dangerous; it doesn't matter to them what is going to happen to the world.

George Bernard Shaw

Rest is not idleness, and to lie sometimes on the grass on a summer day listening to the murmur of water, or watching the clouds float across the sky, is hardly a waste of time.

John Lubbock

I shall be 70 in two months' time and feel exactly as I did when I was 20. I was idle and indolent then, and little has changed in the past 50 years except that perhaps now I am better at getting away with it.

Arnold Thomson

Mind-Lift

When it comes to staying young, a mind-lift beats a face-lift any day.

Marty Bucella

Wrinklies' Wit and Wisdom

In my old age there is a coming into flower. My body wanes; mind waxes.

Victor Hugo

Although I am 92, my brain is 30 years old.

Alfred Eisenstaedt

Anyone who stops learning is old, whether at 20 or 80. Anyone who keeps learning stays young. The greatest thing in life is to keep your mind young.

Henry Ford

We get too soon old, and too late smart.

Dutch

Silver Surfers

TECHNOLOGY

– Mother, are you still on the computer?
– Yes, dear. Sometimes you get into a porn loop and just can't get out.

Edina Monsoon and her mother, Absolutely Fabulous

Here I sit, a modern Werther Original. Not telling dusty fairy stories to my 4-year-old and feeding him teeth-rotting toffees but teaching him how to work my computer so that one day soon he can teach me things.

Peter Preston

A great way to meet the opposite sex when you're older is on the Internet, a good reason to learn to use a computer. The Internet is 70 per cent men, so the odds are definitely in a woman's favour for finding a guy.

Joan Rivers

My nan said, 'What do you mean when you say the computer went down on you?'

Joseph Longthorne

Experts agree that the best type of computer for your individual needs is one that comes on the market about 2 days after you actually purchase some other computer.

Dave Barry

During my 87 years, I have witnessed a whole succession of technological revolutions; but none of them has done away with the need for character in the individual, or the ability to think.

Bernard Baruch

Age and Youth

I am getting older in a country where a major religion is the Church of Acne.

Bill Cosby

When I was young there was no respect for the young, and now that I am old there is no respect for the old. I missed out coming and going.

J.B. Priestley

I'm quite happy about growing older. Who wants to be young? Being 18 is like visiting Russia. You're glad you've had the experience but you'd never want to repeat it.

Barbara Cartland

When I see a young girl I view her with the same pity that she views me with.

Lilli Palmer

We are happier in many ways when we are old than when we are young. The young sow wild oats, the old grow sage.

Winston Churchill

Young people know the rules. Old people know the exceptions.

Oliver Wendell Holmes

I've got things in my refrigerator older than you.

Lee Trevino to Tiger Woods

Old people have one advantage compared with young ones. They have been young themselves, and young people haven't been old.

Lord Longford

Youth is something very new: 20 years ago no one mentioned it.

Coco Chanel, 1971

There's one thing I have over any 21-year-old: a proud history of accumulated neuroses.

Ray Romano

Never have I enjoyed youth so thoroughly as I have in my old age.

George Santayana

Young men wish for love, money, and health. One day, they'll say health, money, and love.

Paul Géraldy

Age is not an accomplishment, and youth is not a sin.

Robert Heinlen

Wrinklies' Wit and Wisdom

This is a youth-orientated society, and the joke is on them because youth is a disease from which we all recover.

Dorothy Fuldheim

All sorts of allowances are made for the illusions of youth; and none for the disenchantments of old age.

Robert Louis Stevenson

I never dared to be radical when young for fear it would make me conservative when old.

Robert Frost

Old age realizes the dreams of youth. Look at Dean Swift: in his youth he built an asylum for the insane; in his old age he was himself an inmate.

Søren Kierkegaard

If youth but knew; if age but could.

Henri Estienne

The belief that youth is the happiest time of life is founded on a fallacy. The happiest person is the person who thinks the most interesting thoughts, and we grow happier as we grow older.

William Phelps

When you are 92 and you say, 'When I was 74,'
it's almost like saying, 'When I was young!'

Ernest Waring

Old and young, we are all on our last cruise.

Robert Louis Stevenson

Mind the Gap

THE GENERATION GAP

Blessed are the young for they shall inherit the
national debt.

Herbert Hoover

Every generation supposes that the world was
simpler for the one before it.

Eleanor Roosevelt

Your modern teenager is not about to listen to
advice from an old person, defined as a person
who remembers when there was no Velcro.

Dave Barry

I used to call anyone over the age of 35, R.F.C.
– Ready For Chrysanthemums.

Brigitte Bardot

Wrinklies' Wit and Wisdom

My son does not appreciate classical musicians such as the Rolling Stones; he is more into bands with names like 'Heave' and 'Squatting Turnips'.

Dave Barry

The denunciation of the young is a necessary part of the hygiene of older people, and greatly assists the circulation of their blood.

Logan Pearsall Smith

The reason people blame things on the previous generation is that there's only one other choice.

Doug Larson

Parents often talk about the younger generation as if they didn't have anything to do with it.

Haim Ginott

There is nothing wrong with the younger generation which the older generation did not outgrow.

Gail Hammond

In case you're worried about what's going to become of the younger generation, it's going to grow up and start worrying about the younger generation.

Roger Allen

The Good Old Days?

In my old age I find no pleasure save in the memories which I have of the past.

Giacomo Casanova

We have all got our 'good old days' tucked away inside our hearts and we return to them in dreams like cats to favourite armchairs.

Brian Carter

I have liked remembering almost as much as I have liked living.

William Maxwell

Reread all the letters you've kept over the years – the wonderful thing is, you won't have to answer them.

Thora Hird

When we recall the past, we usually find that it is the simplest things – not the great occasions – that in retrospect give off the greatest glory of happiness.

Bob Hope

In July, when I bury my nose in a hazel bush, I feel 15 years old again. It's lovely! It smells of love!

Camille Corot

Wrinklies' Wit and Wisdom

One of the oddest things in life, I think, is the things one remembers.

Agatha Christie

In memory, everything seems to happen to music.

Tennessee Williams

– Do you remember the minuet?
– Dahling, I can't even remember the men I *slept* with!

Tallulah Bankhead

– During the …
– If you say during the war, I'll pour this cup of tea over your head!
– I wasn't going to say during the war! Bloody little know-all!
– Alright then. Sorry.
– That's alright. During the 1939–1945 conflict with Germany …

Del Boy Trotter and Uncle Albert, Only Fools and Horses

I never saw a banana till I was 14. I was immediately sick after eating it and haven't touched one since.

Enid Bray

The Good Old Days?

In my day, we never got woken up by a teasmade. We were knocked up every morning by a man with a 6-foot pole … And we weren't having hysterectomies every 2 minutes either, like the girls these days. If something went wrong down below, you kept your gob shut and turned up the wireless.

Old Bag, Victoria Wood

I remember when the wireless was something useful. In my day you could warm your hands on the wireless and listen to Terry Wogan. Nowadays all you can do is listen to Wogan.

Paula Brett

In my day, there were things that were done, and things that were not done, and there was even a way of doing things that were not done.

Peter Ustinov

In my day, a juvenile delinquent was a kid who owed tuppence on an overdue library book.

Max Bygraves

My generation thought fast food was something you ate during Lent, a Big Mac was an oversized raincoat and 'crumpet' was something you had for tea. 'Sheltered accommodation' was a place

where you waited for a bus, 'time-sharing'
meant togetherness and you kept 'coke' in the
coal house.

Joan Collins

Went to see *Macbeth*. We walked out in the
end. Someone said 'womb'. I said to Col – get
your duffle – two pounds on a box of Quality
Street and someone says 'womb' ... It's
happening all over. I mean, in my day, in a
magazine, you didn't have sex, you had a row
of dots.

Nice Lady, Victoria Wood

When you are about 35 years old, something
terrible always happens to music.

Steve Race

At a certain age, you begin to snort at fashion,
you stop going to the cinema and you watch
the black–and–white classic on aeroplanes. You
slouch into a curmudgeonly comfort culture
of the old and familiar, and become a 'call that'
person. Call that music/fashion/poetry/a
chair?

A.A. Gill

The Good Old Days?

Call those pants? I can remember when pants were pants. You wore them for 20 years, then you cut them down for pan scrubs.

Old Bag, Victoria Wood

In my day, men wore driving gloves, women stayed married, and curry had raisins in it.

Swiss Toni, The Fast Show

When I was a child, we took it in turns to have a bath: first the kids, then the whippets, then Granddad.

Ken Dodd

We couldn't afford a proper bath. We just had a pan of water and we'd wash down as far as possible and we'd wash up as far possible. Then, when somebody'd clear the room, we'd wash possible.

Dolly Parton

The older a man gets, the farther he had to walk to school as a boy.

Henry Brightman

In my day, no one had cars. If you wanted to get run over, you'd to catch a bus to the main road … And we didn't do all this keep-fit. We got our exercise lowering coffins out of upstairs windows.

Old Bag, Victoria Wood

Nostalgia is a longing for something you couldn't stand anymore.

Fibber McGee

People say, oh, it's not like the good old days. When were the good old days? In 1900 your doctor was also your barber. 'Say, will you take a little off the sides when you take out my spleen?'

Joe Ditzel

As lousy as things are now, tomorrow they will be somebody's good old days.

Gerald Barzan

If one day you're going to be able to look back on something and laugh about it, you might as well laugh about it now.

Marie Osmond

Always have old memories and young hopes.

Arsene Houssaye

Life

Life is a funny thing that happens to you on the way to the grave.

Quentin Crisp

– I go to the market every day to buy a
  nectarine. At 82, that's life – a round trip on
  the number 6 bus to buy a nectarine.
– That's so sad.
– Not sad. Life. Sad is when you have to mash
  the nectarine with a fork.

Sophia Petrillo and Rose Nylund, The Golden Girls

Life is a moderately good play with a badly
written third act.

Truman Capote

Life is a marathon in which you reserve the
sprint for the end. Mentally I pace myself. I have
got an energy bank account and I can't afford to
be overdrawn.

Peter Ustinov

Two elderly women are in a restaurant and one
of 'em says, 'Boy, the food in this place is really
terrible.' The other one says, 'Yeah, I know, and
such small portions.' Well, that's essentially how
I feel about life. Full of loneliness and misery
and suffering … and it's all over much too soon.

Woody Allen

Life can only be understood backwards, but it
must be lived forwards.

Søren Kierkegaard

Wrinklies' Wit and Wisdom

You only live once, but if you do it right, once is enough.

Mae West

Life is rather like opening a tin of sardines. We're all of us looking for the key.

Alan Bennett

What if the hokey cokey really is what it's all about?

Bob Monkhouse

If logic tells you that life is a meaningless accident, don't give up on life. Give up on logic.

Shira Milgrom

The French Marshal Lyautey once asked his gardener to plant a tree. The gardener objected that the tree was slow growing and would not reach maturity for 100 years. The Marshal replied, 'In that case there is no time to lose. Plant it this afternoon!'

Roland Black

There are only 2 ways to live your life. One is as though nothing is a miracle. The other is as though everything is a miracle.

Albert Einstein

All life is a failure in the end. The thing is to get sport out of trying.

Sir Francis Chichester

I love living. I have sometimes been wildly, despairingly, acutely miserable, racked with sorrow, but through it all, I still know quite certainly that just to be alive is a grand thing.

Agatha Christie

That it will never come again is what makes life so sweet.

Emily Dickinson

The answer to old age is to keep one's mind busy and to go on with one's life as if it were interminable. I always admired Chekhov for building a new house when he was dying of tuberculosis.

Leon Edel

I believe you should live each day as if it was your last, which is why I don't have any clean laundry, because who wants to wash clothes on the last day of their life?

Jack Handey

With whitened hair, desires failing, strength ebbing out of him, with the sun gone down and with only the serenity and the calm warning of the evening star left to him, he drank to Life, to all it had been, to what it was, to what it would be. Hurrah!

Sean O'Casey

Experience

Experience is the one thing you have plenty of when you're too old to get the job.

Laurence J. Peter

Experience is the name everyone gives to their mistakes.

Oscar Wilde

Experience is a comb life gives you after you lose your hair.

Judith Stern

A prune is an experienced plum.

John Trattner

I have learned throughout my life as a composer chiefly through my mistakes and pursuits of false assumptions, not by my exposure to wisdom and founts of knowledge.

Igor Stravinsky

We learn from experience that man never learns from experience.

George Bernard Shaw

If we could sell our experiences for what they cost us, we'd all be millionaires.

Abigail Van Buren

Good and Bad

Old age is a great trial. One has to be so damned *good*!

May Sarton

When you are younger you get blamed for crimes you never committed and when you're older you begin to get credit for virtues you never possessed. It evens itself out.

I.F. Stone

Basil Blackwell said that he had certainly been depraved by the book, *Last Exit to Brooklyn*, but as he was in his 80s at the time the matter didn't seem to be of great practical significance.

John Mortimer

Wrinklies' Wit and Wisdom

What on earth has happened to outrage? There is a hell of a lot in this life to be furious about – and not just things affecting older people – and yet everybody seems to be taking it all so easy. We want more outrage.

Margaret Simey

Old age is an excellent time for outrage. My goal is to say or do at least one outrageous thing every week.

Maggie Kuhn

An 80-year-old man sentenced to 10 years in jail, said to the judge, 'I'll never live that long.' The judge replied, 'Well, do the best you can.'

Anon

Years and sins are always more than acknowledged.

Italian proverb

One should never make one's debut with a scandal; one should reserve that to give interest in one's old age.

Oscar Wilde

Old men like giving good advice to console themselves for no longer being able to set bad examples.

La Rochefoucauld

Don't worry about avoiding temptation — as you grow older, it starts avoiding you.

Michael Ford

Thank You for Being a Friend

FRIENDSHIP

As life goes on, don't you find that all you need is about two real friends, a regular supply of books, and a Peke?

P. G. Wodehouse

We need old friends to help us grow old and new friends to help us stay young.

Letty Cottin Pogrebin

One consolation of ageing is realizing that while you have been growing old your friends haven't been standing still in the matter either.

Clare Boothe Luce

The mere process of growing old together will make our slightest acquaintances seem like bosom-friends.

Logan Pearsall Smith

Wrinklies' Wit and Wisdom

When you're 50 you start thinking about things you haven't thought about before. I used to think getting old was about vanity – but actually it's about losing people you love. Getting wrinkles is trivial.

Joyce Carol Oates

If I had any decency, I'd be dead. Most of my friends are.

Dorothy Parker

The loss of friends is a tax on age!

Ninon de Lenclos

I don't have a warm personal enemy left. They've all died off. I miss them terribly because they helped define me.

Clare Boothe Luce

My only profile of heaven is a large blue sky … larger than the biggest I have seen in June – and in it are my friends – every one of them.

Emily Dickinson

All my friends are dead. They're all in heaven now and they're all up there mingling with one another. By now, they are starting to wonder if I might have gone to the other place.

Teresa Platt

Going, Going, Gone!

DEATH

Like everyone else who makes the mistake of getting older, I begin each day with coffee and obituaries.

Bill Cosby

I get up each morning and dust off my wits,
Pick up the paper and read the obits.
If my name isn't there I know I'm not dead;
I have a good breakfast and go back to bed.

Anon

Why did I not do more in my life, I ask myself, as I read the obituaries of the people who have crammed their lives with 'doing' while I have wasted great chunks of mine dreaming?

Mary Wesley

My old mam read the obituary column every day but she could never understand how people always die in alphabetical order.

Frank Carson

I have never killed a man, but I have read many obituaries with great pleasure.

Clarence Darrow

When I get in a taxi, the first thing they say is, 'Hello Eric, I thought you were dead.'

Eric Sykes

I have been dead for two years, but I don't choose to have it known.

Lord Chesterfield

There are so many ways of dying, it is astonishing that any of us choose old age.

Beryl Bainbridge

There are worse things to die of than old age.

Clive James

How young can you die of old age?

Steven Wright

Hope I die before I get old.

Pete Townshend

I want to die young at an advanced age.

Max Lerner

Statistics tell us that Audrey Hepburn died young. What no statistics can show us is that she would have died young at any age.

Peter Ustinov

Jesus died too soon. If he had lived to my age he would have repudiated his doctrine.

Friedrich Nietzsche, 48

I don't mind dying. Trouble is, you feel so bloody stiff the next day.

George Axelrod

It seems like the only two times they pronounce you anything in life is when they pronounce you 'man and wife' or 'dead on arrival'.

Dennis Miller

– When we die, certain things keep growing – your fingernails, the hair on your head, the hair on your chest…
– Not the hair on *my* chest!
– My dear, you give up hope too easily.

Lawrence Olivier and Edith Evans

For three days after death, hair and fingernails continue to grow but phone calls taper off.

Johnny Carson

Better take my photograph now, dear – I'm 80, I might die at lunch.

Lady Diana Cooper to a magazine photographer

Wrinklies' Wit and Wisdom

At a formal dinner party, the person nearest death should always be seated closest to the bathroom.

George Carlin

I am ready to meet my Maker. Whether my Maker is ready for the ordeal of meeting me is another matter.

Winston Churchill, on his 75th birthday

My family has a propensity – it must be in our genes – for dropping dead. Here one minute, gone the next. Neat. I pray that I have inherited this gene.

Mary Wesley

– How would you like to die?
– At the end of a sentence.

Interviewer and Peter Ustinov

My dream is to die in a tub of ice cream, with Mel Gibson.

Joan Rivers

Let me die eating ortolans to the sound of soft music.

Benjamin Disraeli

I want Death to find me planting my cabbages.

Michel de Montaigne

I shall not die of a cold. I shall die of having lived.

Willa Cather

Errol Flynn died on a 70-foot yacht with a 17–year-old girl. My husband's always wanted to go that way, but he's going to settle for a 17-footer and a 70-year-old.

Mrs Walter Cronkite

– I've decided I want to be cremated.
– C'mon then, Nana, get your coat …

Alfie and Nana Moon, EastEnders

Where would I like my ashes scattered? I don't know. Surprise me.

Bob Hope

I told my wife I want to be cremated. She's planning a barbecue.

Rodney Dangerfield

I've never fancied being cremated or buried. I keep hoping I can hold out long enough for someone to discover some new and more suitable medium for my expiry. Evaporation through abstruse sentence, say. Interment in metaphor. Scatter me in words, O my beloved.

Howard Jacobson

If there wasn't death, I think you couldn't go on.

Stevie Smith

It was Death – possibly the only dinner guest more unwelcome than Sidney Poitier.

Kinky Friedman

Death is nature's way of saying, 'Your table is ready.'

Robin Williams

Dying is a very dull, dreary affair. And my advice to you is to have nothing whatever to do with it.

Somerset Maugham

I'm not afraid to die, honey. In fact I'm kinda looking forward to it. I know that the Lord has his arms wrapped around this big, fat sparrow.

Ethel Waters

Going, Going, Gone!

I'm not afraid of death. It's the stake one puts up in order to play the game of life.

Jean Giraudoux

It's not that I'm afraid to die. I just don't want to be there when it happens.

Woody Allen

Dying is no big deal. The least of us will manage that. Living is the trick. My life has been strawberries in the wintertime, and you can't ask for more than that.

Red Smith

Perhaps passing through the gates of death is like passing quietly through the gate in a pasture fence. On the other side, you keep walking, without the need to look back. No shock, no drama, just the lifting of a plank or two in a simple wooden gate in a clearing. Neither pain, nor floods of light, not great voices, but just the silent crossing of a meadow.

Mark Helperin

What a simple thing death is, just as simple as the falling of an autumn leaf.

Vincent Van Gogh

Wrinklies' Wit and Wisdom

Under the soil, I'll become part of a daisy or a cowslip. To return to the earth will be a kind of reincarnation.

Joan Bakewell

Life is a great surprise. I do not see why death should not be an even greater one.

Vladimir Nabokov

At my age, I'm often asked if I'm frightened of death and my reply is always, I can't remember being frightened of birth.

Peter Ustinov

To die will be an awfully big adventure.

J.M. Barrie

Dying is one of the few things that can be done just as easily lying down.

Woody Allen

I'm dying but otherwise I'm in very good health.

Edith Sitwell

Life is too short but it would be absolutely awful if it were too long.

Peter Ustinov

Going, Going, Gone!

Death in life; death without its privileges, death without its benefits. Who would want that? If you find you can't make 70 by any but an uncomfortable road, don't you go. When they take off the Pullman and retire you to the rancid smoker, put on your things, count your cheques, and get out at the first way station where there's a cemetery.

Mark Twain

I have always admired Esquimaux. One fine day a delicious meal is cooked for dear old mother, and then she goes walking away over the ice, *and doesn't come back…* One should be proud of leaving life like that – with dignity and resolution.

Agatha Christie

We should be more like elephants. When they are dying they creep off and get out of the way.

Mary Warnock, 80

Like a prisoner awaiting his release, like a schoolboy when the end of term is near, like a migrant bird ready to fly south … I long to be gone.

Malcolm Muggeridge

Wrinklies' Wit and Wisdom

– When my time comes, I sure want somebody to put me out of my misery if something tragic happens, like I get a fatal illness or I've lost my looks.
– Just tell us when, Blanche.

Blanche Devereaux and Dorothy Zbornak, The Golden Girls

If I'm ever stuck on a respirator or a life support system I definitely want to be unplugged. But not until I'm down to a size 8.

Henriette Mantel

Euthanasia is a way of putting old people out of their family's misery.

Mike Barfield

My husband died aged 79. He led a wonderful life and never suffered unless I wanted him to.

Suzanne Sugarbaker, Women of the House

My husband died while we were making love. I thought it was funny when he kept saying, 'I'm going! ... I'm going!'

Rose Nylund, The Golden Girls

On Sunday 5 April 1998, following a courageous fight for life, Catherine Thomas

(née Holder) surrounded by family, died at
home – and she's bloody annoyed.

Obituary notice, Cardiff newspaper

When I told my daughter that Edith Evans had
died, she said, 'I don't believe it. She's not the
type.'

Bryan Forbes

George Gershwin died on 11 July 1937, but I
don't have to believe it if I don't want to.

John O'Hara

There is something about a poet which leads us
to believe that he died, in many cases, as long as
20 years before his birth.

James Thurber

The man who invented the hokey cokey has
died. His funeral was a strange affair. First, they
put his left leg in …

Al Ferrera

Martin Levine has passed away at the age of 75.
Mr Levine had owned a movie theatre chain in
New York. The funeral will be held on Thursday
at 2.15, 4.20, 6.30, 8.40, and 10.50.

David Letterman

The inventor of Crest passed away. Four out of five dentists came to the funeral.

Jay Leno

Funeral services were held this week for 82-year-old chewing gum magnate Philip K. Wrigley. In keeping with his last request, Wrigley's remains will be stuck to the bottom of a luncheonette counter.

Jane Curtin

The Chairman of MORI polls has died. He'll be missed by 80 per cent of his family and 35 per cent of his friends.

Craig Kilborn

The Lucky Stiff Funeral Home: We Put the Fun into Funeral.

The Simpsons

They say such lovely things about people at their funerals, it's a shame I'm going to miss mine by just a few days.

Bob Monkhouse

Why is it that we rejoice at a birth and grieve at a funeral? Is it because we are not the person involved?

Mark Twain

This is the last time I will take part as an amateur.

Daniel François Esprit Auber, 76, at a funeral

There's nothing like a morning funeral for sharpening the appetite for lunch.

Arthur Marshall

I always thought I'd be the first to go … Weren't they lovely, them vol au vent. What was in 'em? It was a sort of mushroomy thing. Hey, can I have them when I go, Barbara?

Nana, The Royle Family

I used to hate weddings – all those old dears poking me in the stomach and saying, 'You're next.' But they stopped all that when I started doing the same to them at funerals.

Gail Flynn

In Liverpool, the difference between a funeral and a wedding is one less drunk.

Paul O'Grady

When you're my age, you worry about 2 things – one is when a woman says, 'Let's do it again, right now,' and the other is, 'Who's going to come to my funeral?'

Alan King

Always go to other people's funerals, otherwise they won't come to yours.

Yogi Berra

No matter how rich you become, how famous or powerful, when you die the size of your funeral will still pretty much depend on the weather.

Michael Pritchard

In the city a funeral is just an interruption in the traffic; in the country it is a form of popular entertainment.

George Ade

A stooped old man stood, deep in thought, watching the funeral procession pass by. I whispered to him, 'Who died?' He said, 'The one in the first car.'

Seamus Flynn

Memorial services are the cocktail parties of the geriatric set.

John Gielgud

The trouble with quotes about death is that 99.99 per cent of them are made by people who are still alive.

Joshua Burns

Excuse My Dust

EPITAPH

Didn't wake up this morning.

Epitaph for a blues singer

Did you hear about my operation?

Warner Baxter

I told you I was sick.

Spike Milligan

Let's do lunch next week.

Raoul Lionel Felder

Stiff at last.

Anon

By and by, God caught his eye.

George S. Kaufman, epitaph for a waiter

Surrounded by fucking idiots.

Lindsay Anderson

Afterlife and Immortality

Death is not the end. There remains the
litigation over the estate.

Ambrose Bierce

I owe much; I have nothing; the rest I leave to the poor.

François Rabelais

Almost everyone when age, disease or sorrows strike him, inclines to think there is a God, or something very like Him.

Arthur Hugh Clough

I do benefits for all religions. I'd hate to blow the hereafter on a technicality.

Bob Hope

Life after death is as improbable as sex after marriage.

Madeleine Kahn, Clue

When I approach the pearly gates, I'd like to hear a champagne cork popping, an orchestra tuning up, and the sound of my mother laughing.

Patricia Routledge

Billy Graham described heaven as a family reunion that never ends. What could hell possibly be like? Home videos of the same reunion?

Dennis Miller

Afterlife and Immortality

After your death you will be what you were
before your birth.

Arthur Schopenhauer

I intend to live forever. So far, so good.

Steven Wright

Millions long for immortality who do not
know what to do with themselves on a rainy
Sunday afternoon.

Susan Ertz

If we were promised eternal life we would
shriek for the promise of death.

A.A. Gardiner

If I have any beliefs about immortality, it is that
certain dogs I have known will go to heaven,
and very, very few persons.

James Thurber

Ah, well, there is just this world and then the
next, and then all our troubles will be over
with.

Margot Asquith

I don't believe in an afterlife, although I am
bringing a change of underwear.

Woody Allen

Wisdom and Advice

– Old Timer, I have journeyed far to seek the
  benefit of your immense knowledge and
  wisdom acquired over a long lifetime. Do you
  have any words to share?
– Nope.

Richie Ryan and Methos, Highlander

Wisdom doesn't always show up with age.
Sometimes age shows up all by itself.

Tom Wilson

When I was young, I was told: 'You'll see, when
you're 50.' I'm 50 and I haven't seen a thing.

Erik Satie

From the earliest times the old have rubbed it
into the young that they are wiser than they, and
before the young had discovered what nonsense
this was they were old too, and it profited them
to carry on the imposture.

Somerset Maugham

I was telling my son about the advantages of being over 50. 'As you get older,' I explained, 'you get wiser.' He just looked at me and said, 'In that case you must be a genius.'

Angus Walker

I gave my beauty and my youth to men. I am going to give my wisdom and experience to animals.

Brigitte Bardot

To my extreme mortification, I grow wiser every day.

Lady Mary Wortley Montagu

By the time you're 80 years old you've learned everything. You only have to remember it.

George Burns

Think, man, think … what would Thora Hird do?

Brian Potter, Phoenix Nights

Whenever I'm confused, I just check my underwear. It holds the answer to all the important questions.

Grampa Simpson, The Simpsons

Wrinklies' Wit and Wisdom

I have studied many philosophers and many cats. The wisdom of cats is infinitely superior.

Hippolyte Taine

Since I got to 80, I've started reading the Bible a lot more. It's kind of like cramming for my finals.

Vincent Watson

The whiter my hair becomes, the more ready people are to believe what I say.

Bertrand Russell

Grandfather is the wisest person in the house but few of the household listen.

Chinese proverb

Ask the opinion of an older one and a younger than thyself, and return to thine own opinion.

Egyptian proverb

Trust one who has gone through it.

Virgil

I've been things and seen places.

Mae West

I wish I didn't know now what I didn't know then.

Bob Seger

It is time, at 56, to begin, at least, to know oneself – and I do know what I am *not*.

John Constable

We should be careful to get out of an experience only the wisdom that is in it – and stop there; lest we be like the cat that sits down on a hot stove-lid. She will never sit down on a hot stove-lid again – and that is well; but also she will never sit down on a cold one any more.

Mark Twain

If age imparted wisdom, there wouldn't be any old fools.

Claudia Young

Sometimes one likes foolish people for their folly, better than wise people for their wisdom.

Elizabeth Gaskell

When you win, you're an old pro. When you lose, you're an old man.

Charley Conerly

Wrinklies' Wit and Wisdom

As we grow older, we grow both more foolish and wiser at the same time.

La Rochefoucauld

In the depth of winter, I finally learned that within me there lay an invincible summer.

Albert Camus

H.L. Mencken told me once that he answered all his mail, pleasant and unpleasant, with just one line, 'You may be right.' That's the way I feel now. It is in the realm of possibility, just barely, that I could be the one who's wrong.

Clare Boothe Luce

You stay young as long as you can learn, acquire new habits and suffer contradiction.

Marie von Ebner-Eschenbach

The longer I live the more I see that I am never wrong about anything, and that all the pains that I have so humbly taken to verify my notions have only wasted my time.

George Bernard Shaw

The older you are the more slowly you read a contract.

Leonard Louis Levenson

I am an old man and have known a great many troubles, but most of them never happened.

Mark Twain

I suppose you think that persons who are as old as me are always thinking about very grave things, but I know that I am meditating on the same old themes that we did when we were 10 years old, only we go more gravely about it.

Henry David Thoreau

As I grow older, I have learned to read the papers calmly and not to hate the fools I read about.

Edmund Wilson

As I grow older, I pay less attention to what men say. I just watch what they do.

Andrew Carnegie

It's worth asking: What do you want? It gets harder and harder to answer as you get older. The answer gets subtler and subtler.

John Jerome

I have a simple philosophy: Fill what's empty. Empty what's full. And scratch where it itches.

Alice Roosevelt

One thing I've learned as I get older is to just go
ahead and do it. It's much easier to apologize
after something's been done than to get
permission ahead of time.

Grace Murray Hopper

I seem to have been only like a boy playing on
the sea shore, and diverting myself in now and
then finding a smoother pebble or a prettier
shell than ordinary, whilst the great ocean of
truth lay all undiscovered before me.

Isaac Newton

If by the time we are 60 we haven't learned
what a knot of paradox and contradiction life is,
and how exquisitely the good and bad are
mingled in every action we take, we haven't
grown old to much purpose.

John Cowper Powys

What a wonderful life I've had! How I wish I
had realized it sooner.

Colette

Mottoes to Live By

If you wake up in the morning then you're
ahead for the day.

Mace Neufeld

You can't turn back the clock. But you can wind it up again.

Bonnie Prudden

You're never too old to become younger.

Mae West

It's never too late to be what you might have been.

George Eliot

I think, therefore I still am.

Elliott Priest

If you rest, you rust.

Helen Hayes

You're only old once!

Dr Seuss

Live well, learn plenty, laugh often, love much.

Ralph Waldo Emerson

If not now, when?

Hillel the Elder

Live your life as though your hair was on fire!

Anon

Wrinklies' Wit and Wisdom

Learning and sex until rigor mortis!

Maggie Kuhn

To stop the ageing – keep on raging.

Malcolm Forbes

Never pass a bathroom.

Duke of Edinburgh

Don't take life so seriously. It's not permanent.

Kathy Holder

Exercise daily. Eat wisely. Die anyway.

Anon

May you live all the days of your life.

Jonathan Swift

Live your life and forget your age.

Norman Vincent Peale

May you live to be 100 and may the last voice you hear be mine.

Frank Sinatra

If you can't make it better, you can laugh at it.

Erma Bombeck

He who laughs, lasts.

Mary Pettibone Poole

Index

Adam, Ruth 112
Ade, George 244
Albee, Edward 113
Allen, Dave 49, 189
Allen, Roger 216
Allen, Steve 63
Allen, Woody 21, 22,
    106, 107, 130, 139,
    148, 162, 176, 183,
    223, 237, 238, 248
Altman, Jeff 59
Amis, Kingsley 98, 208
Amison, Phyllis 87
Anderson, Linsay 245
Anderson, Louie 39, 130
Anderson, Susan 170
Anonymous 36, 58, 63,
    76, 90, 96, 113, 121,
    123, 131, 132, 134,
    143, 147, 149, 179,
    182, 195, 197, 203,

228, 231, 245, 255,
    256
Apanowicz, Kathryn 42
Apple, R.W. 33
Arnold, Matthew 18
Asquith, Margot 247
Astor, Nancy 18, 91
Auden, W.H. 85
Austen, Jane 91
Axelrod, George 233
Azine, Harold 103, 104

Bailey, David 74
Bailey-Aldrich, Thomas
    78
Bainbridge, Beryl 97,
    232
Baker, Hylda (*Nearest
    and Dearest*) 88
Baker, Russell 20
Baker, Tom 46, 116

Bakewell, Joan 106, 238, 239
Baldwin, Faith 18
Ball, Lucile 82
Bankhead, Tallulah 55, 106, 218
Barber, Janette 115
Bardot, Brigitte 32, 47, 215, 249
Barfield, Mike 240
Barrie, Diana (*Californa Suite*) 54
Barrie, J.M. 239
Barry, Dave 33, 62, 84, 97, 114, 117, 131, 156, 184, 204, 211, 215, 216
Barrymore, Ethel 83
Barrymore, John 109
Baruch , Bernard 46, 80, 102, 206, 211
Barzan, Gerald 222
Batelli, Phyllis 71
Bates, H.E. 50
Baxter, Warner 245
Beard, Charles A. 101
Beckworth, Harry 117

Beecher Stowe, Harriet 53
Behar, Joy 95, 114
Behn, Aphra 112
Benaud, Richie 61
Benchley, Robert 66, 69, 134
Bennett, Alan 22, 57, 168, 224
Bennett, Arnold 21
Bergen, Candice 70
Bergman, Ingmar 45
Berle, Milton 38, 43, 62, 68, 130, 133, 172, 173, 181
Bernard Shaw, George 85, 129, 209, 227, 252
Bernard, Jeffrey 120
Berra, Yogi 244
Berryman, Lydia 88
Betjeman, John 105
Bierce, Ambrose 245
Birdsong, Wesley (*Lone Star*) 134
Black, Hugo 117
Black, Roland 224
Blair, Lionel 21

Blofeld, Henry 209
Blythe, Ronald 24, 47, 100
Bombeck, Erma 52, 69, 108, 115, 121, 165, 187, 196, 256
Boothe Luce, Clare 229, 230, 252
Borge, Victor 27
Brand, Jo 27
Bray, Enid 218
Breslin, Jimmy 58
Brett, Paula 219
Bricusse, Leslie 104
Brilliant, Ashleigh 84
Brodie, Miss Jean (*The Prime of Miss Jean Brodie*) 26
Brodkey, Harold 108
Brooks, Mel 41, 82
Browning, Guy 92
Bruce, Kenneth 36
Bucella, Marty 209
Buck, Art 98
Burchill, Julie 61
Burke, Billy 16
Burns, George 15, 28, 42, 54, 67, 81, 97, 98, 116, 171, 180, 181, 187, 186, 188, 249
Butler, Brett 77
Butler, Samuel 49, 208
Buttons, Red 47
Bygraves, Max 219

Calkins, Ernest 96
Camus, Albert 252
Capote, Truman 223
car bumper stickers 113, 114, 138
Carlin, George 26, 234
Carol Oates, Joyce 230
Caroll, Lewis 133
Carson, Frank 231
Carson, Johnny 75, 233
Carter, Angela 158
Carter, Brian 217
Carter, Dyson 116
Carter, Lillian 45
Cartland, Barbara 57, 58-9, 212
Casanova, Giacomo 217

Wrinklies' Wit and Wisdom

Cash, Johnny 79
Castle, Barbara 32
Cather, Willa 235
Chanel, Coco 53, 57, 213
Chapman, Graham 121
Chernin, Rose 100
Chesterfield, Lord 232
Chesterton, G.K 105, 147
Chevalier, Maurice 48
Chichester, Sir Francis 225
Christie, Agatha 23
Churchill, Sarah 81
Churchill, Winston 80
Clark, Dick 81
Clark, Frank A. 124
Clarke, Charles 65
Clarke, Cyril 80
Clarkson, Jeremy 60
Claudel, Paul 129
Coatsworth, Elizabeth 104
Cole, Alex 132
Colette 254
Collins, Joan 16, 23, 52, 78, 79, 178, 184, 199, 202, 220
Condon, Jane 115, 116,
Conerly, Charley 251
Connolly, Billy 61
Constable, John 251
Conti, Violet 19
Cook, Peter 68, 10,
Cooper, Sue Ellen 58
Coren, Alan 124, 134
Corot, Camille 217
Cosby, Bill 24, 48, 66, 118, 122, 135, 137, 175, 212, 231
Cottin Pogrebin, Letty 229
Coward, Noël 78
Cowper Powys, John 254
Crane, Frasier (*Frasier*) 30, 76, 158
Crane, Martin (*Frasier*) 30
Crane, Niles (*Frasier*) 76, 158
Crisp, Quentin 96
Cryer, Barry 14, 44

Currie, Edwina 51
Curtin, Jane 242
Curtis, Tony 72

Dalai Lama 134
Dana, Bill 63
Dangerfield, Rodney 37, 41, 65, 66
Daniels, R.G. 62
D'Argy-Smith, Marcelle 16, 128
Darrow, Clarence 231
Dass, Ram 207
Dave (*The Full Monty*) 76
Davies, Hunter 57
Davies, Robertson 101
Davis, Bette 45
Dawson, Les 61
Dead Ringers 32
Decrow, Karen 83
Dee, Jack 64, 12, 125
DeGeneres, Ellen 67
Deland, Margaret 129
Delaney, Shelagh 47
Delany, Bessie 113, 162
DePaolis, Dr Mark 131

Devereaux, Blanche (*The Golden Girls*) 20, 29, 59, 60
Diane (*September*) 51
Dickinson, Emily 96, 225, 230
Diller, Phyllis 19, 45, 55, 68, 75, 121, 144, 159, 175, 183
Ditzel, Joe 222
Dodd, Ken 66, 124, 221
Donne, John 53
Dorothy (*Men Behaving Badly*) 174
Drabble, Margaret 101
Dwyer, Bill 131
Dylan, Bob 34

Eastwood, Clint 93
Edel, Leon 225
Einstein, Albert 107, 198, 224
Eisenstaedt, Alfred 210
Eliot, George 255
Eliot, Thomas Stearns (T.S) 21, 32
Ellerbee, Linda 79

Ephron, Delia 70
Ertz, Susan 247
Esprit Auber, Daniel
   François 243
Everage, Dame Edna
   118, 160, 161

Faith, Adam 71
Farrow, Boyd 31
Feather, William 90
Fellini, Federico 71
Fellowes, Julian 48
Ferguson, Marilyn 123
Ferrera, Al 241
Fields, W.C. 107
Fierstein, Harvey (*Torch
   Song Trilogy*) 51
Fischer, Martin H. 118
Fisher, Carrie 100
Flaubert, Gustave 99
Fleming, Richard 71
Fletcher, Bert 87
Flynn, Gail 243
Flynn, Seamus 244
Fonda, Jane 54
Forbes, Bryan 241
Ford, Michael 229

Forster, E.M. 105
Forsyth, Bruce 43
Fowler, Gene 47
Foxworthy, Jeff 84
Foxx, Red 70
Frankfurter, Felix 33
Freiberg, Jim 67
Freud, Clement 28, 95,
   98, 111, 129, 140
Friedman, Kinky 236
Frisch, Max 32
Frost, Robert 27, 214
Fry, Stephen 87, 111,
   113, 116, 150
Fuldheim, Dorothy
   214

Gabor, Zsa Zsa 12
García Márquez, Gabriel
   42
Garcia, Jerry 73
Gardiner, A.A. 247
Gary (*Men Behaving
   Badly*) 37
Gaskell, Elizabeth 251
Geldof, Bob 117
Géraldy, Paul 213

Getty, Estelle 110
Gielgud, John 128, 244
Gilbert, W.S. 20, 57
Gill, A.A. 220
Ginott, Haim 216
Giradoux, Jean 237
Glenn, John 27
Golden, Ronnie 35
Goodman, Ellen 27
Gordon, Richard 120
Gores, Joe 46
Granger, Anna 114
Grayson, David 108
Green, Jeff 42
Greene, Coral 86
Grey of Falloden, Lord 93
Grimes, Maud (*Coronation Street*) 112

Haber, Karen 115
Hadley, Joe 87
Hammond, Gail 216
Handey, Jack 225
Harper, Chris (*Calendar Girls*) 49

Harper, Valerie (*Chapter Two*) 52
Hathaway, Katharine 31
Hawn, Goldie 25
Hayes, Helen 34, 255
Healey, Denis 125, 200
Heinlen, Robert 213
Heller, Joseph 84
Helperin, Mark 237
Henie, Sonja 79
Hepburn, Katharine 17, 88
Hernu, Piers 60
Hicks, Seymour 35
Hill, Harry 62, 125, 146
Hird, Thora 102, 136, 192, 217
Hockney, David 55, 127
Holder, Kathy 256
Holt, Victoria 109
Hoover, Herbert 215
Hope, Bob 46, 68, 110, 178, 217, 235, 246
Horne, Lena 88
Houssaye, Arsene 222
Howard, Lillian 104
Howe, Ed 18, 20

Wrinklies' Wit and Wisdom

Hubbard, Elbert 81

Hugh Clough, Arthur 246

Hugo, Victor 210

Huston, John 107

Hutchins, Robert M. 69

Huxley, Aldous 85

Irving, Washington 36

Isherwood, Christopher 104

Jackson, Holbrook 84

Jackson, Sally 56

Jacobson, Howard 236

Jagger, Mick 31

James, Clive 91, 232

Jerome, John 253

Jones, Jennifer 51

Jones, Tom 74

Jong, Erica 99

Jordan, Barbara 102

Jowker, Ron 41

Kahn, Clue, Madeleine 246

Katz, Jonathan 94

Kaufman, George S. 245

Kavet, Hebert J. 40

Kay, Peter 86, 87

Keillor, Garrison 40, 92

Kelvin-Smith, Paul 36

Kemp, Martin 63

Kemp, Millicent 39

Kemp, Rowena 41

Kierkegaard, Søren 214, 223

Kilborn, Craig 242

King, Alan 66, 243

King, Jan 120

King, Stephen 85

Kirchenbauer, Bill 130

Kornheiser, Tony 63

Kranz, Judith 77

Kringle, Kris 15

Krouse Rosenthal, Amy 67

Kuhn, Maggie 228, 256

Landers Ann 89

Landis, Martin 138

Larson, Doug 66, 85, 216

Laufman, Lois L. 45

Layton, Ralph 44
Leacock, Stephen 130, 163, 168
Leary, Timothy 80
Lee, Gypsy Rose 56
Lefkowitz, Louis J. 81
Lehrer, Tom 18, 21
de Lenclos, Ninon 230
L'Engle Madeleine 105
Lennon, John 22
Lerner, Max 21, 232
Lessing, Doris 93
Lette, Kathy 20, 29, 51
Letterman, David 28, 64, 71, 72, 73, 74, 75, 90, 111, 118, 164, 188, 204, 241
Levenson, Leonard Louis 252
Leyden, Michael 44
Lichtenberg, Georg Christoph 208
Liebman, Wendy 61
Lionel Felder, Raoul 245
Lipman, Maureen 91
Llewellyn, Susan H. 39

Lloyd, Harold 18
Longford, Lord 213
Longthorne, Joseph 211
Loren, Sophia 53, 68, 70, 80
Lorenzoni, Larry 28
Lubbock, John 209
Luks, George 96
Lynn, Janet 52
Lyttelton, Humphrey 17

MacArthur, Douglas 44
Maden, Geoffrey 43
Madison, Oscar (*The Odd Couple II*) 118
Maher, Bill 126
Mainwaring, Alan 42
Manning, Bernard 99
Marsh, John 38
Marshall, Arthur 95, 243
Martin, Rose (*The Golden Girls*) 43
Martin, Steve 93, 101, 119
Martinez, Lydia 19
Marvez, Monique 59

Marvin, Lee 91

Marx, Groucho 17, 34, 44

Mason, Elsie 87

Mason, Jackie 89

Matthau, Carol 47

Maugham, Somerset 83, 236, 248

Maurois, André 33

Maxwell, William 217

Mayhew, Sandra 59

McCartney, Paul 22

McErlane, Maria 38

McFadden, Cyra 77

McFarland, Jack (*Will and Grace*) 18

McGuiness, Ross 122

McLaughlin, Mignon 19

Meiklejohn, William 71

Meir, Golda 47

Meldrew, George (*One Foot in the Grave*) 29

Meldrew, Victor (*One Foot in the Grave*) 29, 39, 111, 190,

Melly, George 23, 55

Menicus 85

Merton, Mrs 65, 115, 120, 133, 138, 161, 174

Merton, Paul 62

Meynard Keynes, John 107

Midler, Bette 56

Milgrom, Shira 224

Miller, Annie 162

Miller, Arthur 106, 109

Miller, Dennis 233, 246

Miller, Henry 201

Miller, Jonathan 69

Milligan, Spike 245

Monkhouse, Bob 31, 82, 119, 126, 181, 190, 224, 242

Monsoon, Edina (*Absolutely Fabulous*) 51, 114, 210

De Montaigne, Michel 235

Moon, Alfie (*EastEnders*) 235

Moore, Christopher 40

Moore, Patrick 30

Moran, Dylan 65
Morley, Christopher 128
Mortimer, John 14, 45, 46, 69, 92, 116, 117, 122, 182, 227
Moyers, Bill 206
Muggeridge, Malcolm 92, 239
Muir, Felicity 94
Murray Hopper, Grace 254
Murray, Jenni 113

Nabokov, Vladimir 239
Nash, Ogden 30, 125, 192
Nearing, Helen 34
Needham, Richard 89
Needham, Sean 90
Nesbitt, Rab C. 31
Neufield, Mace 254
Newton, Isaac 254
Nicholson, Jack 79
Nietzsche, Friedrich Wilhelm 84
Norden, Denis 39, 40, 42, 66, 95, 102, 123, 186

Norton, Dorothy 94
Nylund, Rose (*The Golden Girls*) 58, 64

Oberon, Merle 80
O'Brien, Flann 121
O'Casey, Sean 208, 226
O'Hara, John 241
Olivier, Lawrence 233
Ono, Yoko 72
O'Rourke, P.J. 48
Osbourne, Ozzy 73
Osmond, Marie 222
Ozick, Cynthia 50

Pagett, Eloise 207
Paige, Satchel 15, 16, 17
Palmer, Lilli 212
Parker, Dorothy 27, 230
Parton, Dolly 53, 63, 81, 163, 221
Pearsall Smith, Logan 22, 57, 216, 229
Peel, John 87
Perelman, S.J. 118
Perls, Dr Thomas 83, 123

Peter, Laurence J. 46, 226

Petrillo, Sophia (*The Golden Girls*) 59, 60, 67, 126, 127, 132, 135, 156, 159, 198, 223

Pettibone Poole, Mary 256

Phelps, William 214

Phillips, Bob 25

Phillips, Julia 33

Phillipson, Prue 49

Picasso, Pablo 17, 85

Pierce Adams, Franklin 24

Pilates, Joseph 37

Platt, Teresa 230

de Poitiers, Diane 18

de Portago, Barbara 53

Porter, Cole 79

Pound, Ezra 95

Powell, Anthony 29

Preston, Peter 211

Priest, Elliott 255

Priestley, J.B. 91, 212

Pritchard, Michael 244

Proops, Greg 75

Prudden, Bonnie 255

Quant, Mary 20

Queen Elizabeth II 125, 151, 157

Queen Mother (Queen Elizabeth) 151-3

Rabelais, François 246

Race, Steve 220

Raleigh, Walter Alexander 110

Ransome-Davies, Basil 41

Raphael, Frederic 71

Reagan, Ronald 106

Redford, Robert 77

Reed, Lou 73

Reith, John 109

Renwick, Clidd 74

Reynolds, Burt 65

Richardson, Julia 60

Richter, Jean Paul 93

Rivers, Joan 15, 21, 30, 54, 55, 60, 75, 77, 211, 234

Roach, Hal 119

Robbins, Mitch (*City Slickers*) 26

Robson, Lottie 40

Rochefoucauld, La 228, 252

Roddick, Anita 76

Roosevelt, Alice 85, 253

Roosevelt, Eleanor 215

Rosenberg, Leo 132

Ross, Deborah 50

Routledge, Patricia 246

Royle, Barbara (*The Royle Family*) 56, 86

Royle, Jim (*The Royle Family*) 56,

Rubinstein, Helena 19

Rudner, Rita 75

Russell, Bertrand 250

Ryan, Richie and Methos (*Highlander*) 248

Sainte-Beuve, Charles Augustin 32

Santayana, George 213

Sarton, May 227

Satie, Erik 248

Saunders, Jennifer 33

Savage, Lily 50

Schary, Dore 25

Schofield, Mark 40

Schopenhauer, Arthur 247

Scott, Zachary 109

Scott-Maxwell, Florida 94, 103, 159, 198

Seger, Bob 251

Seinfeld, Jerry 24, 59

Seneca 105, 128, 168

Seuss, Dr 255

Sexton, Anne 23

Sharples, Ena (*Coronation Street*) 111

Sherrin, Ned 131

Shulman, Milton 44

Simey, Margaret 228

Simmons, Michael 112

Simpkins, Larry 90

Sinatra, Frank 256

Skelton, Red 35

Slater, Colin 37

Smith, Betty 54, 100

Smith, Dodie 52

Wrinklies' Wit and Wisdom

Smith, Hannah 128

Smith, Martin and Millicent 86

Smith, Red 237

Smith, Rev. Sydney 207

Smith, Stevie 236

Smyth, Ethel 53

Sneddon, Brenda 86

Solomon, Dick 61

Spark, Muriel (*see also* Brodie) 108

Stair, Nadine 107

Stark, Freya 100

Steele, Edna 87

Steinem, Gloria 99, 132

Stengel, Casey 22

Stern, Judith 226

Sternen, Lilith (*Frasier*) 157

Stevenson, Robert Louis 214, 215

Stone, I.F. 227

Stone, Sharon 70

Stoppard, Tom 84

Strauss, Kurt 38

Stravinsky, Igor 227

Street-Porter, Janet 112

Stritch, Elaine 14, 78

Sugarbaker, Women of the House, Suzanne 240

Sullivan, Frank 50

Swift, Jonathan 256

Swiss Tony (*The Fast Show*) 221

Sykes, Eric 232

Taine, Hippolyte 250

Taylor, A.J.P. 100, 102

Taylor, Elizabeth 82, 95

the Elder, Hillel 255

Thesz, Lou 135

Thomson, Arnold 209

Thomson, David 72

Thorpe, Adele 38

Thurber, James 22, 241, 247

Tony (*Men Behaving Badly*) 62, 160

Top Tips (Viz) 60, 64, 121

Townshend, Pete 232

Trattner, John 226

Trevino, Lee 213

Trotsky, Leon 45
Trumpington, Baroness 97
T-shirt slogans, 46, 110, 112, 134
Tucker, D. 35
Twain, Mark 22, 50, 67, 69, 81, 82, 135, 239, 242, 251, 253
Tyler Moore, Mary 89

Unfaithful, Mary 86
Ungar, Felix (*The Odd Couple II*) 118
Ustinov, Peter 28

Van Buren, Abigail 227
Van Gogh, Vincent 237
Van Slyke, Helen 23
Vaughan, Bill 31
Vincent Peale, Norman 256
Viorst, Judith 55, 94, 183
Virgil 250
Volkart, Edmund 46
Voltaire 99

von Ebner-Eschenbach, Marie 252
Vonnegut, Kurt 36
Vorse, Mary 208
de Vries, Peter 127

Walder, Angela 127
Waldo Emerson, Ralph 255
Walker, Angus 120, 249
Walker, James 120
Walter Cronkite, Mrs 235
Walters, Julie 114 (*Baby Talk*) 149
Waring, Ernest 215
Warnock, Mary 239
Waters, Ethel 236
Watson, Vincent 250
Wax, Ruby 16
Webber, Miles (*The Golden Girls*) 43
Webster, John 96
Weinstock, Lotus 206
Wendell Holmes, Oliver 23, 45
Wenz, Sheila 76

Wrinklies' Wit and Wisdom

Wesley, Mary 231, 234

West, Mae 75

Wharton, Edith 103

Wilde, Oscar 20, 51, 52, 69, 80, 88, 226, 228

Wilder, Billy 35, 162, 163

Williams, Harland 76

Williams, Robin 119, 133, 236

Williams, Tennessee 218

Wilson, Flip 108

Wilson, Harold 84

Wilson, Jack 43

Wilson, Mary 26

Wilton, Mavis (*Coronation Street*) 207

Winters, Shelley 16

Winton, Dale 70

Wodehouse, P.G. 15, 109, 133, 229

Wogan, Terry 126, 191

Wolfberg, Dennis 98

Wood, Victoria 41, 79

Woolf, Virginia 99

Wortley Montagu, Lady Mary 49, 249

Wright, Jerry 83

Wright, Steven 17, 29, 126, 127, 147, 232, 247

Wynn, Harriet 88

Yeats, W.B. 101

Young, Claudia 251

Youngman, Henry 119, 125

Zbornak, Dorothy (*The Golden Girls*) 20, 29, 127, 132, 156, 173, 176, 179, 240; (*Empty Nest*) 48

Zbornak, Stan (*The Golden Girls*) 64

Zola, Emile 101